THE UNFINISHED BREATH

new poems, elegies and laments

Volume One

Iván Argüelles

LUNA BISONTE PRODS
2023

THE UNFINISHED BREATH
new poems, elegies and laments
Volume One

(Written October 21, 2021 – May 1, 2022)

These poems are dedicated to the faithful memory of Max and Joe, whose unfinished breaths remain a part of the Continuum.

"forsan et haec olim meminisse iuvabit"
Virgil, Aeneid, I, 198

© IVÁN ARGÜELLES 2023

Cover and book design by C. Mehrl Bennett
VOL. ONE ISBN 9781938521911
VOL. TWO ISBN 9781938521928
https://www.lulu.com/spotlight/lunabisonteprods

LBP

Luna Bisonte Prods
137 Leland Ave
Columbus OH 43214 USA

THE UNFINISHED BREATH

para Arturo Dávila

is it possible the universe has no beginning ?

non-stop and all in *italics* the sequence of *Booms*

reaching from as far back as Minnesota to the Olmec ruins

poetry is just an incremental inch in the deathless cycle

one starts here and moves the chess piece to the side-walk

over there even as the traffic turns to glass

opium is big as a perfume ! and the naked ladies

who boast of Caucasian lovers and alcohol

at nine in the morning when darkness seethes

and the ignition ! it is a ceremony in wax

by noon the destroyed work will be a mere hologram

riddling the content of cosmic diction with acid rain

by ten minutes I missed being first !

and gazing at the stars visible by day all three trillion and eight

what a somber occasion counting is

if one could but remember all the numbers in order

paralyzed and belittled by our own minds we are just digits

offerings to the furnace of Desire !

names begin to fail as does the courage to move on

so slender the waist of time and fading

bullets puzzle the invisible fabric of thought

amazing skies fold in on each other the perplexity

being human is just trash ! to supersede the *other !*

there is a cordillera that leads all the way to the embryo

the fuming disregard for rock and uninhibited matter

supine structures of abandoned syntax

the evolution of light from a thread of water

the origination of Number from nothing and

countless heroes named after galaxies

do we march with our heads carried underarm ?

to look and see absolutely nothing ! air !

the purple hills of distance are alive with Spanish dialect

forensic pleasures hidden in ocelot skins !

to the south further than ideas can travel

lie the lawns of the fabulous dead with their hummingbirds

and serpent sounds sculpted from pure intransigence

there are twins and more twins equally absent !

and the homophone of the blackest Aztec sun

everything is pervaded by disorder

rains and dizzy spells and the violent traffic

of Avenida Insurgentes ! the gravel of sleep

and the invisible Wheel of perpetuity

that never *moves*

10-27-21

THE BRIEF HAZARD OF LIGHT

movement and gravity the only day of thought

wordless sleep of the eons when rock and tumult become

the cemetery of space that cavernous adolescence

spent in corridors of pre-geological oceans

ear to the shell of flame the dictionary of smoke and

resin where remembrance deposits its first and second

instances of desire the rainfalls of pittance and shale

what matters the third day of infinity ! sections of

unavoidable air thicken in a debate of storms

ships set sail for the fourth time across drums

of iridescence and rumor and the whole fabric

the penance of galaxies and noise seconds in the making

before the entire repercussion prepares for rebirth

cinder and gravel roiling in a grief of dreams

the phantom frigates that require the number five

and ports of no known entry flash and disappear

in the insane panoply of a Homeric mind planning

to invent verse and the execution of shorelines

pre-dawn scintillations of passion the fingers of

an ethereal deity with horses of pure black sweat

that plunge through solar homophones irreverent and

mutilated with hunger for mortality ! other ciphers

uncountable asterisks inkblots parenthetical vowels

issues of granite and morphine the destitution of cities

built in tens one upon the other like tissue papers

it is never today ! hand gropes for hand in a quicksand

of rhetoric and fever and six times the polar zero

circles itself in a horrific rendition of *time*

seven is the consonant designed by the Mayo clinic

and eight is the diphthong that erases memory !

nine is the day we all gather in high school & it's always
Friday morning and everyone is still alive !

10-29-21

ELEGY FOR *NIKKI ARAI*

I don't know if there is a natural order to poetry
no more than there is to grass growing wild
in an ant's memory nor stone lifted to its zenith by
a proportion of sleep no more than there are vowels
excised from an Etruscan mirror or a depth charge
loaded with x-rayed consonants the verbiage of Sumer
and Akkad ! what happens are words untrammeled
in a fugue of passion and error followed by grief
which is the summit of human rumor and the skies
that discharge the remnants of a previous universe
confetti of azure sands and photographed gravel
what occurs are the discordant sounds and harmonies
of a hypothetical noise lodged in rock formations
which are the ear's innate archaeology and speech
which is the redundancy of what statues recall every
noon when the court-house cannon fires its salvos
deep into the promise of hills and twilight dialects
sorrow mourning longing hieroglyphic registers

that flicker in the dream's prolonged homophone
and when darkness confirms its fists of finality
and night corroborates the cycle of astral heat
a syntax of plunging bodies Asiatic in size and
smoking one last cigarette before the ambulance
with its shadowy beings in negative enlargements
of a past love affair encounters in an afternoon
bar redolent of bad perfume martinis and tobacco
the irises in their derangement in cracked vases
shoved into a corner and the jukebox loud with
refrains of repentance and tears pouring madly
from betrayed eyes and it is then poetry appears
no better than an allegory of regret and mistakes
cribbed verses from a dead-end adolescence and
nostalgia for the unpossessed goddess of *oblivion*
such as it is the poem suffers its hiatus and
simply vanishes in rush hour exhaust fumes

10-29-21

VERTIGO

the full conjecture of rumor and sound
navigating the oceans wary between the eyes
double the accident the world of the unseen
forest lost mind abandoned without direction

traveling with the dead to errors of space
remembrances of a single afternoon and hills
and dialects of grass and hidden exits
to the south spirit-realm of the unknown
riddled with echoes and misspent vowels
talk of stone and abyss the immense seas
that exist only to avoid detail and tempests
and human cries in the midst of punctuation
between galaxies and before the origins of time
the rebirth of sorrow and footfalls and waters
coming up to the edge and the repercussions
of image and taunt in a late version of language
everything occurring simultaneously on
a moving Chinese screen patterns of air
and winds that rip ears from their song
dreaming bodies that emerge and float and
divide along fault-lines with desires to hold
what has no substance and the pure enmity
persisting in the darkness that defines mortality
Buddha eyes intent on fixing the point of no return
somewhere in the depths left behind by mountains
that have lifted from their immobility to fly
into sanctions of ether and sheer distance
afterthoughts of becoming and vanishing
the small noise of communication that only
bees can understand *vertigo*

10-31-21

DÍA DE LOS MUERTOS – 11/4 (JOE & MAX)

i

Brooklyn a park bench a quart bottle of

malt liquor and a brother

how did that happen late spring early death

drone of skies ready to annihilate themselves

an ear wrenched from its rock formation

a buzz of intonations from the Mahatmas

stoned and iridescent in their vanishing

perched like quetzal birds on the telephone wire

high above planet Nothing all comes back

to this moment realization of these deaths

the masks of infancy withering yet beautiful

and Hey ! did you hear the eloquence emanating

from the jazz trumpet of Miles Davis ?

basements in accolades of marijuana smoke

decadence and livelihood waiting for births

for nomenclatures to disclose their irate vowels

in a backyard next door to Betty Carter

mind soaked in tequila playing boyhood one

Last Time and it all falls down the sudden repetition

of a life experience the onset of seizures

the rest of *breath* reduced to a red parenthesis

inside which the conflagration of ideas and love

recycled eerie representations of store windows

masked and hooded figures demons alluring

and baleful and after that what is there to know

a trip to the outback a dozen hospitalizations

mysterious tumors ventilators bad x-rays

memories of Mayo Clinic cold spells

long periods before and after that no one remembers

but for the poignant high notes the small echo

in its shell and the massive but absent seas

ii

the little red clarinet case pushed under the bed

sheets wrung out turning yellow from ichor of the gods

transpiration and head-wounds tilted off the moving

wagon on to the sidewalks of inferno and whatever

could that mean the isolation wards and always

the stranger at the door bare-knuckled with a bag

to capture whatever malignant spirits trying to escape

the maps were drawn tight around the peninsula and

causeways and trampolines for the kids to jump

up and down inside the *coma* where an excised cosmos

auto-destructs with all its plastic passengers

most of whom have traveled to the Yucatan and

harbored nights in Teotihuacan with vessels of ether

the countdown hasn't even started before the finish

is a fait accompli the forlorn hills of dialect and

twilight the way they reappear in dreams half-beings

bereft of intellect and side-swiped by planetary diesels

plunging like headless horsemen down the Pan-Am Highway

motels and endless waiting rooms dismantled telephones

ambulances and more ambulances the wrong address

and finality of sliding curtains hanging like angels

left to dry from the wars and the doctors of hypnosis

and mercury just staring into the abyss devoid

of language the cuneiform of their brains working

overtime to excuse themselves from all culpability

and soon it's another Halloween trick or treating

on the doorsteps of a missing basement and phantom

music ascends *The Monster Mash* with c*alaveras de*

azúcar and the jingles and marionettes of memory

dancing sing-song in the cavities

I got the shakes I'm going fast

iii

cada día es el día de los muertos

11-01-21

FOR *MAX* LISTENING TO *THE MONSTER MASH*

Dear One! you fled too soon there's enough

air and light and space in the atmospheres

for a hundred of you and yet all those

markers along the road the baseline off

by three centimeters the misquoted speeches

of recent bodhisattvas all in gravel and rubble

the hyphenated portions of biology and trust

it's all a scramble to define the world's mess

aggravated attempts at flight angelic and

soaring notes off the scale in a music that

requires no ears simply the echelons of sleep

the intaglios and niches where souls hide

remission of doubts and hectares of innocence

subsumed in the earthly snares of poetry and

error the constant reassembling of vowels

the consonants that are the basis of cliffs

and maelstroms and however much the crickets

lodged in memory's small shell resound with

heat and passion and the grasses lay down

their invisible heads and the fields teem

with ghosts of adolescents who never "made it"

just as you ensconced in your ten-year old

cocoon grappled with the concept of the years

the fuming passage of the unseen thread through

immobilized calendars counting up to forty

and then came the famous blank revolver

aimed at the source of echoes deep in the lake

of unfathomable thoughts miniscule and unheard

like the rains coming down hard against windows

that only faced out onto the vanishing cosmos

11-02-21

THE DAY AFTER NIBBANA

Buddha nature in hibiscus and nasturtium

in bird-song before dawn in cricket-strum

echoing heat in summer fields built of memory

in shuttered rooms cloisters of renunciation

in trellis vine and tiny white budding in the shade

a house too distant for capacity and winds from

mountains blown to erase mortal passions

in accidents of alcohol and mechanical design

in deaths and orphans and new-bride widows

in books that imitate shop-windows and girls

who have just learned the *secret* and combs

and braids and playful finger tosses of a ring

the vicious and the plenty the unkempt and

the holy each tipping the scales of emptiness

curvature of space and denial of time the logos
and its antithesis the forgetfulness of vowels
in clouds that scour remote universes for
a chance to be born again and skies multiplied
by a single integer of wings and whatever a child
dreams before he goes to sleep and grasses and
weeds and hands that live hypnotic lies like
mandarins and bonzes who burn their souls
to avoid the body and its constant eerie shadow
Buddha nature in the error of human thought
the breach of consciousness in trees and rock
the absolution of language and its tinderbox
of refutations in the systems of cognition and
plastic toys and salt and great eras of quartz
the histories re-told a thousand times on the back
of a tattered postage stamp the noise and rumor
of wheels at night and gravel trembling in its
veil and so many other matters of no concern
that shudder like fireflies trapped in their screen
and delusions above all that life is real the next
best thing to dying and breath and x-rays and
small bleeding animals left to wonder always why

11-03-21

THE SERMON AT RAJAGRIHA

the text unraveled the scope becomes unclear

life's finest breath taken and returned to its echo-

source lights flicker like distant asterisms that

eye no more beholds and memories once radiant

a longer doom-spell enfolds how lush curtains

of air the dawn received greeting lustrous but

unseen souls phantoms on the gyre of troubling

fate all in a rush undetermined the confused

moment of give and take when vowel and homophone

resound in the inner ear and cascades of water

luminous liquid consonants of a language only

statues in their noontime quest for sound perceive

understanding embroidered in leaf and grass

histories of mortal lust and combat entangled

in the opaque clinic of the senses hand and foot

bound to a reticence of betrayal and the gods !

splendid in their unfathomable punctuations

simply waste their glances on the world's loose

dissent and error for why this mistaken

gravity this weight that encumbers shoulder

in its myth of strength and nymphs do dance

their naked noise and splash the invisible with

mirages of stealth and dominion that entice men

folly to pretend to *know*! enigmas and secrets

that involve the mystery of stone and rumors
of heavens and clouds that gain on sleeping
darkness the queen of the vault and her maids
emblems of flashing thoughts swift to disappear
in earth's tumbled shadow embrace of embryo
and sepulcher the myriad and more than many
illusions of matter and nerve gesso and repartee
of distances twilight dialects and mountain slopes
on the other side of time ! the unknown and vast
which is the greater of the multiple hemispheres
in which consciousness dissolves its tiny lamp
& islands of memory simply sink into the mere

11-04-21

THE SHIBBOLETH OF POETRY

this mistake this graven image this metaphor
of flame and enticing hearts this boudoir of memory
pleasure-filled with naked arms white with chalk
and distances of a goddess too primed to realize
the hand falters in its ink of sigmatic resonances
and houses big and empty and the dalliance of light
metamorphosis ! words to plunder noises and ears
the waters that scheme underfoot and grasses

that cling to tongues of waxen skies the legends

of hermetic truths but carmine blusters on the wave

handsome marble hewn in imitation of a deity

whose invisible nonsense meant to inspire only

creates imps emboldened to walk the wire

and fall and fail and clouds that loom before high noon

and lamps and switches and vocalic sensations

ampersands of tombs and moving pictures darkening

as the nocturnal streets of ire and ancient sands

huge memories invent and amorous prisons and

retention of a single kiss that implodes in books

and illustrations of lipstick and eye-liner and hair

foils and combs and the clinic around the corner

where drugs play to fool the human mind with sounds

that seem like lyrics and the syllables that disinter

adolescent loves in fields of burnt corn and rye

insects ! the brain implies a labyrinth of beauty

and endings to a universe that came and went

inside a verb for make-believe spelled in lobbies

of libraries as wide as afternoons and voices

of the unfound dead whose poetry of repercussion

continues to be written in a mirror-script

and read aloud to butterflies and hummingbirds

and other fantasies of winged imagination

shibboleth ! mechanics of desire and death !

11-04-21

IN THE REALM OF THE SENSES

the strange and narrow field that vision fuels
with projected matter lives and woods and airs
clouds the very substance of sleep and disordered
minds that attach to nothing the whole of thought
origination and suspension repercussion and self
everywhere the dizzy apparatus of sight the blind
are fortunate to discount and overwhelmed by
memory the confused mask assumes an ego and
forth plunges into the mire of cities plans and maps
a text of strategies for the forlorn and disabled
of heart that love dismays and wonderment of night
the asterisks of illusion and fateful noise of spheres
mists the brain and raining light from secret spaces
the world enlivens for a moment before augmenting
dark the earth embraces and hover we still in small
assays to understand ignition and its varying flares
ideas and tropes of unlit hemispheres colliding
daily in the unknown and what of *us* the statues
quickened by some rare breath to succumb again
to disease and aspirations yet tumble walls down
and lawns escape the fired salvo of noontime blows
the chemist and his panderer by the corner wait
to stage their plays enticing adolescent passions
to mount displays of vertigo and amniotic recall
remembrances of sound in the buried ear and rock
and cliff climbing into invisibility the skies behind

childhood's efforts to overcome and delusions of

flame the smoking effigies of photograph and quartz

linger the pronouns designed by fate and oblivion

with its finely jeweled crowns and strike the iris

that divides the sun's blackening homophone into

unequal shares and die repeatedly the bodies

given over to desire's surfeit of mirage and spite

at once ! the end to what never was begun !

11-05-21

CINÉMA VÉRITÉ : NATALIE WOOD

truth to behold the knees first and following

the spine up to the back brain where convulsed

the actress resumes a former identity in black-

and-white clearly obscure a fiction in imagery

hair loosely set sailing in Zephyrus' contours

and boarding a roadster of pure quicksilver

steps on the gas heading straight for the cliff

of despond a Socratic delusion fueling the ear

lacking speed for a song but dimly remembered

the sands and grit of oblivion picturesque as

a backdrop of steep mountain azure and climax

the accident only inferred rounding the proverbial

bend foot on the accelerator imitating the gods

in their nonchalant suicides one after the other
can hear the loud and the symphonic decibels
a vowel at a time until the consonant clusters
gathered like a hair-piece to fit an empress is
it any wonder the full screen version with its
anatomy of painted viscera and bone-tissue
declamations of statuary in the clarity of noon
do then clamber for survival the lesser parts
bit roles played by adolescent blinded by rage
or the passion to suffer as Adonis on the shores
of distance and coming back into relief the auto
speaking Italian this time and waving a white
glove into the fantastic embroidery of air she
winsome almost unclad steering her motor
out of its mind and the ignition with thoughts
of fire and water elements of creation ! even
as the camera angles its obsolete vision under
the wheels and gravel takes its nocturnal course
nostalgic for windows and the fray of lamps
in the upper floors just barely glimpsed
as the mechanized chariot pulls into its garage
months after the electricity has failed again
and shots ricocheting in the ambiguity of time
will not understand the leaf in its origin
nor the way grass succumbs to the night

11-06-21

JOE WITH WHOM I STILL SLEEP

para nuestra hermana Laurita

suffer great longing and separation today

taking refuge in some dark Himalayan dialect

while the mind is still driving its car through

by-lanes of youth twin-speech fragmented

in broken skies of mirror transcendence

how much happened how much did not happen

occurrences of leaf and murmur the ear in its

ocean of solitude and grieving for noises lost

the utter as much as I can recall of what was

born with me a hank of hair the upper lip a-

tremble the spirit-talk of statues listing in

a stream of light far off to the left of the map

of the radio lasting moments of eternity on

a floorboard knees down and eyes fixed on

a geometry of distant galaxies no more than

inches from the border of sleep and to have

none of that back to be in retreat from the real

the deaths in all their subtle detail of playgrounds

kicking balls of dust into the sun's remote sound

whose is the brother that can't come home where

is the window where darkness keeps its boys

and wall-paintings of islands desolation and

baying of secret hounds to lie down against

the pane and remember without any recall

the designs of grass and star-bright gravel

a wheel rounding its own Mexican infinity

which of the two of us is doing the fandango

of meaningless words the pointing to *this* but

meaning *that* and waiting as always for mother

to bring us to light some fateful winter day

the moorings and tapestries of the womb

heralding the moment when one of us must

go first finger lost in grassy twilight and cry

the must and dregs of an alcohol that sets

like a planet on the rim of an unknown house

we will transport one another from school

and down dusky alleys write whole books

about the hours and symphonies we shared

without knowing how absent we already were

11-06-21

HARMONIC CONVERGENCE :
WHAT IS THERE IN THE ABSENCE OF SPACE?

floating through the space sleep creates without number

no words that form thought no sense of the loss of feeling

the mind a vacuum in which the body dissolves all

contour in the imagination of asterisks and phonemes

nothing but the noise of an invisible chaos stirring

in an ear of dust vacancies of light the famous *unknown*

the swiftly moving stasis of the unborn in quanta

navigating aimlessly in the playground of the dead

aspirations of continents to reshape themselves loud
and infinite and the revolving eternities of a single
day that extends in all directions without beginning
and without end the hand shattered in possibilities
of creation and dissolution the former is the latter
the topmost rung is in the basement of the gods
burning without smoke and colder than planet Pluto
the head is an infirmity of its own making a rock
of cognition and recall a vowel outside consciousness
looking in on itself traveling with motionless galaxies
through immutable constraints of light and disorientation
the mountain on one side is the same as the one that
cannot be seen beyond the echo of roiling waters
waking is as inevitable as the ensuing pact of oblivion
ledgers and shifts of hues and domains of distance
falling is the constant and time is the measure of lack
we surge out of a moment of pure sound advertised
as the Big Bang and yet there is no memory no nostalgia
nothing but unspoken longing and its unheard music
shadows all appearing to move against walls of silence
without motivation toward an enigmatic resolution
--death the stopwatch and pulse unpredictable dice
smaller images beneath the lens the hours ants compute
to harvest rice legends of fingernails and blues-notes
the always unkenned unfathomable moment called
eternal-return without remembrance or design *night*

11-06-21

THE SUPERFLUITY OF DAYS

no consolation the small light that discloses

an illegible text on the waking margins of cognition

the anticipation of a day growing from memory

of dew and cascades of orient and the lesser

divagations of mountain and endlessness among

the mythographers who anthologize vowels

reticence of the obverse of coins depicting

emperors wearing the Asiatic wounds of ancient deities

the hiatus glimpsed in their eyes of deserts

that rise like ant-hills overnight and to succumb

to the least detail of smoke the convergences

of flame and grass a conflagration in the ear !

to wander in the repetitions of childhood going

over the denounced birthright with its cuneiform

noise about just who when and where and the skies

multiple now and ceaselessly threatening

what does it mean *"another day"?*

confess the sentence can never be concluded

by the staccato emphasis of the brain to comprehend

even as the shoulder sorrows its burden and

hills of opaque distance for the knee to overcome !

walking in the circular infinity of the critical moment

harboring disciples of innocence and defeat

inside their cracked windows of wintery grief

come ! too many hours and weeks have passed like

a hologram of the sun rising for the first time

illustrated on the pages of a storm yet to come

to bed then and night with its numinous stalkers

who return with repercussions of speech

dreaming we will come to life again

11-08-21

THE CARDBOARD COFFIN

for Alexander

while Max in his cardboard coffin slept all the ships

left port slipping into a small celestial lake that reflects

the errors of other worlds and planets composed of dew

the letters printed on his coffin refused to fade

even as the rising smoke offered possibilities of a distant realm

and still the plaintive echoes of the painted air

held discourse with consonants and lightning bolts

like rumors that wheels make circling the rare infinities

of fragmented rock and pine-cones in the dust

then Max began to disappear into a number

that they failed to count a cipher prepared at birth

when the margins of human conscience turn to wax

for the secret flames that burn like solar alphabets

spelling words unknown in the shapes of clouds

that die at sunset when night recycles its dim lament
and asterisks and sparkling dots and pinwheels
made of fireflies scour the darkness for a reason to exist
and the stifled cries of insects in the fevered heat
and the silent moans of fishes in the liquid deep
while Max in his cardboard coffin slept a brief eternity
dreaming the world he left behind was but a plastic toy
meant to circle the cosmos in the minutes of a day
then as if yawning Max took his coffin by the flimsy lid
and with it vanished into the brimming saffron air
where continents of atmosphere and separate heavens
search for perfect entities in the vestibules of outer space
while here down below hummingbird and butterfly
make patterns of invisibility and dusk in the memory
without hemispheres beyond the south of time
and all the things that could have been

11-09-21

THE TWO DARKNESSES

one is made of inarticulate mind the other
a paragraph that envelopes all of space
two darknesses that govern birth and death
the in between is a forest and some houses
by the side where lamps struggle to open

to the disappearing air and give motion

to the gravity that cannot move and some

times a cry is heard and others silence overwhelms

the Buddha in his chrysalis gives signs of

renascent thought then regrets the noise

of so many increasing worlds that issue

from desire's single spore

these darknesses walk with us through all

the days of memory and still we value

nothing more than to vanish before their

night draws to a close and finds us dumb

on the other shore

we looked for each other in the dense swarming

listening for the hand that pities stone

and simply settled for the finger

missing in the grass to realize our year on earth

was but a fumbled guess a step taken

out of turn between the doubled dark of time

and the emptiness it defines

11-09-21

ARISTOPHANES & BECKETT

is this a comedy with no last act?

is this a comedy with no last act?

if the soul continues to persist in all

its hemispheres of rebirth and intoxication

then salvation becomes a dead letter writ in red

the bylaws of a superficial universe of opposites

dualities of vowel and solar homophone

disunity and tautology of a single consonant

designed to end the realm of speech and if

and if and if the cosmos has no beginning

it will never end and this comedy we play

each a role of ego and denial wearing masks

we cannot pull off at night sleeping in clouds

of gilt and rust and longing for an end to time

we dive into one another's dreams and

totter on the edge of the self-same knife

and the soul if it is ever to be free and the body's

fatal but repetitive illusion will one day dissolve

in the compact of light and oblivion

then what need is there for this comedy

for these theories of act and interlude for this breath

and leaf and pantomime of becoming One

again and again the flawed and ageless text

recited in recoil and pentimento on a stage

of gamma rays and pure dissonance planets

unto ourselves plunging in and out of sound

wordless noise of conjecture and symbolism

adolescence eternal mind-games of memory

libraries at day's end where lessons are expunged

of meaning and illustrations turn to blank

signatures of love and obsession wavering

on the last page of a script that was never edited

an isotope a convergence of insect and cuneiform

to read with eyes shut illegible confessions

of gods who have existed only as syllables

in a Pythagorean history of transmigrations

of insomnia and respiratory distress

to wake ! shadows of hands and nothing more

silhouetted against crumbling stucco walls

11-10-21

THE FAILURE OF LANGUAGE

empty realms of the senses the clock is ticking

for the hundred and nth time we and they both

the world's fragrances its ephemeral floral delicacies

the world's stench its floods and augmenting deserts

for you and me both the pronoun is to no avail

sections of the jagged continent fallen off

eruptions of underwater lava and porcelain

deities that have lost their heads monsoon and

solar homophone bursting ultraviolet ambulances

paramedic and pharmacist gigolos of imbalance

the time has come and gone to make a decision and

at the top of the ladder smoking his last desperation

in a cigarette targeting the red headed Magdalene

the final Christ surfaces in someone else's dream

an advertisement for sandalwood soap a neon

version of Achilles or Adonis the shore beyond

the shore is vanishing and the Boatman haggard

and annihilated by the riot of human noise tilts

his oar in the Stygian murk weighing the consequences

of conveying syllabic corpses vocalic shells hiatus

and circumflex punctuations of history the adjunct

phallus and emblem of the soul wayward and drunk

as ever flitting between cadavers in a ballet of chance

and election the frizzy haired girls on the boulevard

spike attitudes in their drinks solipsisms of logic

even as the rage of weather and distance destroys

the mountain's immense capacity to fly and

dialects arise in the suborned hills of twilight

a choice of Plato or abandonment practiced in

a syntax full of imploding asterisks yes even as

the world in its diaphanous moment of self realization

prepares to embark on its last journey backwards

through time taking with it the tool-shed and anchor

the galley proof and chisel adapted for the cuneiform

that puzzles cliffs and arroyos late at night

consonants of stuttering abdication and cognition

the brief attempt to make light and breath endure

the child ! the fossil trilobite and flushed anemone

glowing pink and iridescent in the cancer ward

the failure of language ! the failure of language

to mean to make sense to argue truth to save the world

divagation of mispronounced caveats and legends

of judgment and deformation aphasia and amnesia

it is the you and me the misplaced accent the fourth tone

sliding into the abyss the little squiggles erased dots

flash cards resurrected phonemes celestial and infernal

the *not this again* and agonizing over the repetitions

and repercussions and the totem beasts the junk

entire cities lost in sigmatic inflexions ! retrograde

and infinitely soundless grammar of space

global warming heat and ice endless rains and

the failure of language to correct anything !

10-11-21

"NEVER TO RETURN AGAIN ! BE HAPPY !"

hung in the sky neither moving nor falling

the objects and senses of the mind

occlusions of thought the inward pulse

to far flung galaxies immobile as pharaohs

laid to rest in their enigmatic hieroglyphs

was it to understand pattern and cliff

to design at day's start an imperceptible

heaven unattainable even as the motors

without keys begin their license to act

marauding streets issues of texts unfolded

in the midst between harvest and drought

the sooner the celestial bodies are realized

and cartoon effigies immoderate in proportion

to the size it takes to reduce the sun's noise

to the small echo in an ear-shell and do then

learn to fly rock and sleeping clefts tones

aggravations of memory inserted sidewise

by noon the cannon thunders its once in

lifetime and the courthouse built of a single

stone shakes ever so and the girls combing

their tresses and pouting in the noon-glare

will a drug tease them back to shape ?

so much happens in an instant and thudding

deities of recoil and tempest the afternoon

introduces sections of future in grasses

and shades the structure of oblivion dark

turning the corner to the photo-mat to

pose for a five-and-dime shot to grace

the cover of a magazine and the evening's

new drum resounds sending shattered kids

to the palladium of excess and electricity

uncontained music asterisks distances high

and loud already asleep the world on its

emptied wharf adrift in silhouettes of water

the intangible poetry of longing and leaves

lengthening hours between the trees

which are witness to tragic accidents and

roulette of reason spare intimations of

afterlife as a possibility in dusky gloaming

a sadness that accompanies wayward

the passage home the darkening pronoun

and as ever the personas of evidence

flickering lamps in the remote windows

and to bed the ancient grieving loss

11-12-21

IN THE YEAR OF THE JUBILEE 1300

lost in a post-classical world of dialects
obscure as the woods they inhabit leaf-rustle
and twilight of distance tarnished metals ocher
and fade golden russet trembling flashes between
eye-glance and torpor steeds swart and glistening
with sweat and cadavers and talking mules the route
littered with fragmented mile-stones illegible epitaphs
Greek finger-cups shattered in the ear's ghostly
decibels like sleep in a sky looming thunderous
as caverns and grottos the unwinding thread the skein
the lion that devours its own shadow and men
who are a pantomime of straw figures and
speech defects in poetry transmuted vowels
systems of opaque reference to dimly remembered
choral preludes or a suite of incongruous hexameters
set down for a psaltery and early cembalo flutter
of harp and lute resonance of hands stroking notes
in descending order to the ladder that holds
the ocean and the terrible baying of hounds in the midst
of an unfinished tale the woman bound to a rock
the hero blind evanescent fire-brand approaching
stealth of consonants confused and deictic shifts
the steps leading to a cathedral in the shape of Mary
emotion choked artifices ringing timely hours
the feigned and actual diseases saturating the night
with poisonous fumes the adders of consumption and

distress with no way out of the labyrinth of root
and branch mangled corpses still walking bearing
weight on a crooked staff mewing and bleating
of unseen creatures the heart dense with terror
how it ends how it can end the marvelous signals
pre-dawn warnings muffled cries spirit entities
circling like halos the stone effigies erected
as if by magic before the Duomo and chronicles as
defamed as they are true the passage of souls from
seed to kinglet fierce etymologies of cloud and dew
the constant divagation of the heart to sing !
umbratile names jongleurs and troubadours
restless spurs and cordwain saddles and ringing
afternoons in reverie of the Unseen Lady of Tripoli

11-13-21

THE BURDEN OF MEMORY

great the sun slashing windows wide open today !
if only the street could remember and the houses
side by side with coffin-bearers and the slopes
that lead nowhere up and trees amazing and glorious
with secret knowledge on all levels with leaves
that talk and see and the hosts of winds and vowels
in the very air bright and suffused with solar texts

but to have to recall every word every sound every noise
the footfall in the flower plot the finger lost in grass
the rattle of the mower in the shadows by the willow
and plum and stucco and brazen emphasis of light
where children play with their own ghosts gaunt
and haggard in the passage of a day before everything
goes up in billows of red and saffron powders which
are the obscurities of a universe that devours
itself nightly and the comic strip characters who
come to life and kidnap babies before noon and
of all places in Mexico City large and brawling
with Toltec dialects in the colorful marketplace
and enormous histories of spit and combs and pack
animals forced to do the job of men writing endless
lies the mentation and language of a higher cognition
every day is the same day ! memory is a cyclone
taking the years in their entirety and convulsing them
as we age the distances become short circuited and
schoolyards are curtailed and put into cuneiform footnotes
I am nothing but a tier of ascending notes to a song
without words and my family members are stooped over
in hot fields picking harvests long overdue and it is
only the minutes of a lost hour that have to be counted
before death at last riding a small red tricycle
appears in a wavering mirage across the street

11-13-21

VARIATIONS ON A HOMERIC THEME

on the fourth floor of the department store

an unbearable music announces the goddesses

in whose hearts burns the destruction of Troy

it's the holidays the great green fir hangs upside down

and kids and noise and tinsel make festive song

despite the slow burning of the Trojan citadel

Apollo's angry with Athena both shake their

bronze pleated spears and shout high notes that

shatter the distant glass in porticos of smoke

school's been out a long while and the yearbooks

photographed and sealed & outside the weather map

looks bleak and stormy and cars go speeding

into the fierce night of poetic battle and verse

still the fourth floor of the department store shakes

with foot-stomping dance the annual sophomore ball

girlfriends line up for a kiss and the boys hide out

in corners drinking fast booze and the goddesses

irreverent as valkyries pound the steamy air

with fists like festooned pompoms and floral grace

the world's a lark a haven for poets with dreamy

stares and the escalators move up and down humming

intransigence and fate and toys are traded for

guns the license to kill is open sport for all

Hector bids farewell to wife and child and struts

galore into the fray his brother handsome Paris

tarries lingering far behind with a host of Greek names

vowels and consonants suitable for window dressing

it all comes back to study hall and books opened

to colored maps of time and the riot and echo

of the Olympians who speak a Latin cribbed from

interlinear translations and love if it could only

bloom in the ratty papered notes that spell *Mary Lou*

and the seasoned lattice work of stars above and

yes it's all a spiel of memory a bout with grief

endemic to all who have been born to tryst and

vie with goddesses in whose heart flames an end

to innocence and the wintery shores of distance

where raging seas of oblivion beat senseless rocks to dust

and in my heart a mind to die for all the disappeared

the girls lined up for kisses like forlorn fireflies

and the boys embraced by the booze of death

in the Sixth Book of Homer's Iliad

11-14-21

A VEDIC HYMN

dusky steeds driving between the atmospheres

just as thought waking penetrates then goes

lost in the mists somewhere between the eight

peaks of earth the three heavens the distances
and the seven rivers mind's agglomeration of
consonants retroflex and surd the divine axle
molten gold that informs the sun's dark homophone
all of creation suspended between the hidden
vowels of the year 1300 BCE and an oriental
display of waters layered in triplicate x-rays
the fundament of reason a sidestep in waning
light comes evening and the asterisks and dots
electrified by right pronunciation and stress
of sounds coming into order and the house
of Being and its thousands of illumined rooms
and darkness too the awnings and parasols
to fend off despair and the demons and sorcerers
disguised as plenitude and shadow the furious
evocation of the interstices between life and
death breathing correctly laying the stone in
its place by the fire and circumambulating to
the right then to the left the place where the
Invisible one stands giving direction and focus
to the Unknown which will one day be manifest
reflecting back and forth between numbers
never to exceed Three ! the enormous paths
to be taken if only the correct one was designated
and mortals now in the billions half starved or
living in drought and warfare the deserts of

history the fantastic multiple cities arrayed one
on top of the other burning ceaselessly and
smoke signals of language to no avail if but
to understand the original words the coupling
of noise and meaning to raise the hands to
the fleeting airs of sky and the clouds numinous
and roaring with ancient sleep

...

who will protect us and speak for us now?

11-15-21

FROM THE HIGH LOFTY SKY A VOICE

understanding memory the roots deepen night
archaic blooming astral houses filled with noise
screens adrift over boundless waters shifting hues
anachronisms of light investing planets in serial
deaths plunging matter into holograms of ether
panoply and grief sorrowing thought aching for
release the entire mess of light and breath leaf
and grass rock formations slowly moving through
an alternate space echoes nostalgia and longing
waking when there is no reason but despair
quickened by depths too proximate for hope

sensational moments of ecstasy followed by crimes
against the mind mortals vying with immortals
poetry and dissent the enormous hiatus between
sound and meaning strutting Greeks blind rishis
gopis wet with discomfort abused in their separation
from the Master whose flute playing hypnotizes
beast and bird making stones to sing utterly mad
eclipses of thought recycling mandalas of flame
through the eye ! it is and always has been this
one single moment turning on itself in a fixed
gyre of emotion and truant passions kaleidoscope
vision with hands reaching out everywhere and
to suppose this is eternity reduced to its thumbnail
whatever happened before yesterday cancels out
the frequency modulation tomorrow is reckoned
to be and we lift ourselves for an instant from
the improbable surface of experience only to fall
back into the abyss pronouns misplaced masks
divergent follies of cognition and rumor hearsay
of philosophy cliff and rebuttal of existence
the evanescent *all*

11-16-21

LANQUAN LI JORN SON LONC EN MAY

it's bright morning early light flush

I am on Riverside Drive close to the year

1300 *anno domini* and I am to meet Dante

tonight in a Greenwich Village bar and I am

tag-ends with the megrims hung-over and

polluted with bad everything in my veins

but a lark is in my brain and singing in its

own small Latin the sonorous verses of

Jaufré Rudel and life ! is big and important

I can see New Jersey through the fogs of

impermeability and easy death and horns

and sirens what do I care youth is in my

shoulders and my knees are driven by verse

traffic is beyond velocity and I dare step

to the right before moving through time

so the day before yesterday is really tomorrow

and I have a new job mending books in

a basement at Columbia University and I

have stolen a small book of Provençal from

the stacks and hope to impress Dante when

I recite from memory *lanquan li jorn son lonc en may*

and if I step even further to the back of space

then I am really on verge of completing my

eighty third year and Dante must be tired

of waiting down in the *Café Wha?* nibbling

on shrimp cocktail and feeling the blues

over remembrances of Beatrice all of thirteen

if not younger and how will I get back to that

point in time in Morningside Heights not far

from the Unicorn tapestry in the Cloisters

so much is yet to happen or has already happened

to know which I can't discern but that young

and bold and actually dumbfounded with ego

I scribble on the back of some leaves great

brilliant new poetry in the manner of Guido

Cavalcanti and the *dolce stil novo* emotions

and words I have cribbed and made my own

strutting forth in the imaginary atmospheres of

lovelorn forsaken crusaders embarking on

lifetime's only adventure to create and to love

how suddenly alone I am and the concrete spires

the glass technology of sky the architecture of

the archaic air with its clouds racing towards

Washington Square and New York University

where I am studying Lucretius with Lionel Casson

whose specialty is ancient ship-building and to

hail Venus in the first pages of my unwritten

book and in a trance standing there with motors

and novelties whizzing too fast to see and an

individual takes off his mask and points to

two women across the street one is named Asia

and the other remains nameless and they

stare into the profound depths expecting me

to understand their symbolism and soon

a gong sounds and bonzes in burning saffron robes

who are sick of history and a voice from

the other world advises to abandon language

in a quandary I needle through dangerous

hours and look for a resort in Greek myths

Theseus of course and I will discuss this with

Dante tonight if I ever get that far

11-17-21

THE LIMITS OF KNOWLEDGE

the unfinished layers of light yet elude

no one ever completes the goal the absences

illusionary moments of eternity unfocused as

the axles melted and the steeds exhausted

fell to the winnowing floor and whose loud suit

and aviator cap kept shining despite the dark

ensuing hills and dialects of dissension far

to the outback of a lost continent drifting

south of the crematoria and the piloted texts

of the later Roman Empire and did arise

a figure in eights and threes imminent for

its mythographic mask the plenary shadow

the object lesson in use of the honorific pronoun

obscenities cast aside the ditch and its fears

how many the rush of memories in the recycled

sound and subterfuge of the grasses bent

in the night shaft of winds and lesions the far

stars and asterisks and unlit candles wavering

cloud-forms without substance names erased

in the lengthening list of mortal failures grief

and lamentation around the corner and kids

6 feet in all directions slamming metal shields

against the imposing architecture of air and

glee-shouts rendered nil and void the onslaught

of chemistry and adolescence approaching pools

where echoes wait for the summons and fueled

by masks of deceit and promise a legend of

nymphs and death and what else is there ?

11-18-21

WHITHER ?

the weight of the passing days though finite is

heavy and interminable the remembered sorrows

the imminent grief the realm of unseen tempests

anxieties brought to the curbstone and tethered

like solar stallions left to idle in the vacant

homophone abandoned by the cycles of heat

and injustice that characterize cosmic histories

and you ask of me and I ask of you *whither ?*

each dawn fraught with old tales from the morgue

antecedents of ambulance and lawnmower going

over landscapes and dialects of dissent we have

become invalids of life wounds that have never healed

the rose and the canker sore and the evening news

can we not get over *that ?* alarms and fossils

we bear in our sleep with great enmities of light

folded over and under clouds mushrooming in

preterit dreams the small escape valve of language

what good does correctly punctuated syntax have ?

it is in the wards where aphasia reigns where loss

and longing assume the size and shape of leaves

that words become nothing more than random noise

sounds uttered and reiterated and put to the page

and finalized and turned into texts that none can read

history in all its illegible pornographies tiny glyphs

scribbled in vanishing ink before our very eyes

and I ask of you and you ask of me *whither ?*

both scorn and tenderness attend emergencies

nothing abates the mistaken clause the hiatus for

no reason at all the glottal stop and the chasm

we turn to windows blinded by the late sun's trial

remains of warmth embers of memory slipping

away into the blank interstices of a calendar

that has no dates but a sequence of question marks

the hierophant who spoke in riddles was right !

11-19-21

SOLITARY MAN

the dust has settled planetary and otherwise left

standing alone me with my dulcet aching grief

hidden and secret to the world as it rounds dangerous

as never before the bend cinematic anguish to close

the door on the crypt sealing within phantoms

the dear ones to my heart fragments of the greater

rock that stands outside of time the answer is Yes

going back exhuming memories making them walk

again substantive components of unjust deaths

micronaut and mandala-designer the fictions of

breath and antinomy the legacy of summer lawns

sprawling around a single June afternoon and splash
and orient and sorrow all within the keep of an unseen
tower guardian slowly moving by my side up the path
to the mystery that governs the heights with grass
and leaves that talk and bleed at will before darkness
spreads its night-spell and the glister and clutter
of asterisks spawned in the theater's ceiling beguile
am I to render the self to attrition and insomnia
aphasia of the errant thought juxtaposed to the glass
where rotating figures spin their eights in phosphorescence
cannot be returned the encomia and prejudice of being
and alone beneath the spectral solar letter stripped
of my pronoun the ominous delusion that tomorrow
is a possibility finger pointing to the hedge where
the other of me the double the copy whom I resemble
is there waiting for the moment of cosmic explanation
a bible of truant thumbs inches of a similar text
sounds translated to their nearest equivalents in
the language of trees roots and hieroglyphs of silence
the one true communication before the fabric of
outer space auto-destructs in vapors visible only
in dreams that someone is having about me
out there somewhere profile of negative light
diminished and vanishing to the southland where
a solitary man surrenders vestige and shadow to
the already gone whose brother looking over the shoulder
whispers *where have you been all these years ?*

11-19-21

ABRACADABRA

what will make us whole ?

who will regulate the course of the sun ?

who can explain the library ?

if one hand falters is the other to blame ?

what is the impact of a drop of water ?

no answers only taunts and jibes of seers

blind and fumbling to open the envelope

a word is a rock a sound the patterns of air

meaningless and void before the ominous oracle

what is an island without the seas ?

aging swiftly youth surrenders its skin

to the sudden extension of light

hair fails to expel the fading alphabet

the shape of gold and its addiction enchants

theaters of envy and malice open their doors

who is the uncanny gate keeper ?

to understand the epic of trees listen to the split

in the earth from which arise mephitic thoughts

anguish of the day to locate its planet

endless rotations of the thumb in its orient

in which of the many rooms does memory hide ?

we are left with stone puzzles graphs of sky

silhouettes in glass with resemblances to us

copies of redundant shadows moving

in the archaic distance of grass

resonance of the ear in its loss of symmetry

placing the head somewhere between the leaf

and its disorder and aphasia

are dreams the attempts of silence to break ?

like rows of insects departing the darkness

of their birth and insistence to move

we shift in chaotic syllables out of schools

into long playgrounds of hiatus and chance

soon deaths are upon us mechanical and vibrant

diesel motors and repercussions of flight

aerial oceans elevated by philosophers

in search of the truncated truth

asking always asking which of the four Vedas

contains the most assonance and of the rules

for living in the forest or pronouncing

without digression from the original noise

all is dissent of mountains and imperfection

metallic forces hidden dangers loss

twins are a clue to the unities

but nothing more and sorrow

who will be the last to tell ?

going is an inconvenience

and the fatal echo of language and

the greater ambiguities

11-20-21

WHAT IT WAS LIKE BEING A TWIN

not just dying a little bit more to the shadow

accompanying the music of alleys after the rain

but with cup and sword to embrace the opposite

on street corners with all directions bright with

promise to do better next time shoring conclusions

at the Jobs' Daughters dance the darkening couplets

ravenous with a diction of sheer incomprehension

like swarms of night insects blazing to become extinct

the powerful of wish and thinking it makes otherwise

the sonant gold draining from the back-brain a fuse

or a letterhead in gilt suffering between fists the knee

on the afternoon pavement and stones placed in

their separate hemispheres so echoes have to part

like dice in the random spell of eternity reflected

back from the drug-store's plate glass window we

stopped precisely there to savor infinity's first

blow watching traffic and exhaust fumes hit the sky

what was the yelling but the song to belong outside

routine to be as the pyramids in the southern tropics

a course in linguistics between five and ten stores

the passion was on us to learn flight patterns wingless

and grieving the imminent loss and as the rubber

skidded away from the great invisible wheels that

plied the destinies of photography and aphasia

subjects acquired in shelving library books after school

the Latin predicates the totem beasts of Yucatan

illustrated versos of imperial numismatics a hand

followed by its context we began to understand dichotomy

and its absolute empire between Vedanta and Heraclitus

pushing the edge to its margins in a space unexplored

zygote ! two is as a far as it gets the ensuing three

can be the highest quotient and the chemical tables

puzzling with quiddities of the number *red* was to believe

and spread the map out on the green baize spectacular

for the city-plans of noise and idiom the vowels implied

a form of justice and could hear the ear's profound shell

taking in the lacquered oriental seas with Chinese fleets

about to discover the Old World and aching to know

but never understanding and cognition and the small

knot to untie before going to sleep forever as Joe did

11-21-21

THE INCONCLUSIVE CIRCLE

in memory of Philip Lamantia

Dawns ! how many of you are left to shine ?

plangent oriental dew-drops fleck like constellations

the mental rim and the source of light cognition

to elevate the senses a last time and draw in

the unachieved weeping that defines any mortal

the tree-bowered hill that must be climbed

in order to find the Friend and his map

awkward translation of the numinous text

of memory the ancillary planets stopping to rest

by the side of Highway 52 and the court summons

shirts on backwards pantaloons and rafts

the stagecraft of talking shadows the willowy

lengths of girls tittering behind the curtain

only they know the *secret* but in their haste to

get to the drug-store have forgotten what it was

waist and hip shoulder and knee bruised by

gravel of the pharaohs strewn before the midway

echoes no ear can apprehend the sobbing sad

as a lifetime can be the imminent betrayal

news that time has run out that the Greeks

cannot set sail again that Iphigenia's longing

is of no consequence and it is always after school

the sun declining past the meridian the Bosporus

grown sleazy purple in the diminishing lamp

silks and rumors of other worlds somewhere

after the bell has rung and the western apocalypse

with trainloads of barbarians thumbing their Baedekers

pages of alternate facts dime-store princesses who

have perpetuated hourly excursions in the park

to feed the spotted deer of the Vedanta only

to listen for the far-off language of salvation

grammar of calamity and woe night spreads its

starry grief and glitter all too soon with galaxies

dead these thousands of light-years ago

POETRY IS A FAKE illegitimate red sounds

the ventriloquist's orient duplicated and copied

in 18th century photomats seclusions and repeats

of a distant mountain where hidden metals apply

their fuse to the canned laughter of emperor Caligula

road bound to a helioport with tons of vowels

ready to implode in the rhetorical imitation

of the Argonautica super dense and infirm

straddling the eternal aqueduct that leads to

the baseless southland residential complex of the dead

immobility of the Hour of constant repetition

SHIVA ! hundreds of hundreds and nothing more !

and the Dawns with their ushered suits of chrome

and instability and the endearments of gods

left to dry out in morgues where futility is a language

clouds and remnants of the day before time began

and boomerangs that talk ! a consonant that can

never be redundant and the mind in its bedlam

never forwards never back isolation and aphasia !

11-22-21

IT ALL HAPPENS AT ONCE

the chrysalis from which we emerge the flower

the critical waters of sleep depths entirely

of the mind chasms and abyss cities in mirrors

smoke dun-colored hills rituals of ignition

and tapestry the world turns on its tilted pole

ready to burn captured by the error of duality

feminine and plural the circling storms the airs

the atmospheres the painted clouds the distance

to the next celestial body the sun's black homophone

rumors of previous existences words and lanterns

the very dialects of absence and memory myths

shaped out of vowels gone out of use and sounds

never heard before that limit thought from

exceeding the speed of light situations of childhood

small fossils laid to rest chambers of innocence

annihilated by the *unexpected* witless fuels and

ampersands the leveled mountain and its orient

beds of saffron and matrimonies of rock and height

silt gravel loam mulch decaying beauties of writ

and testimony of faked histories backside of metal

sheer epiphanies of noon when shining is widest

and the constant drill of breath the hope and loss

of everyday collisions that cannot be accounted for

elements on the chemical table feasts of noise

within the ear's dormant shell the hallucination

and warp of realities shadowed and reflected in

broad avenues of glass given to a traffic of insects

fields of camphor and passion *heat!* delivery systems

of skin interpolations and adolescence of language

next to nothing the fatal note the crescendo and digit

of the unheard melody pyramids and brothers

buried in a single grain of sand the rout of lipstick

in the dark fission and centrifuge of wrong-thinking

in the end all the little letters that spell nothing

wavelength and diptych this one minute of eternity

11-23-21

WHO DO WE THINK WE ARE ?

it is not to present the self as any special thing

a pronoun without embellishments abnegation

and doubt unskilled in resentment lacking envy

asking not for extension of breath but to understand

at last the limitations the abyss and its otherness

frayed edges longing and loss of control the absences

which have become the greater portion of existence

the seas that come running to take the knees away

as such sky is a blasphemy and clouds and rain

and thunders that strike without presentiment the

meters and rhymes of a lost poetry semiotics of despair

rituals of the morgue enticements of bedlam and

utter silence cast off vowels the repercussions that

remain of sound the atmospheres loaded futility

to go on is only to emphasize sheer loneliness at

the end the fatal inch of the hand to cease moving

grasses and missing fingers and ears asleep as stone

the aching and grief that define and the fierce

memories that keep repeating and bedside nightfall

lamentations of leaf and stucco the draining away

of the waters disappearance of mountains and shadows

whatever happens next whoever approaches the diameter

an immense size will occur and ink and aphasia and

the dominant structures of air and myth voices from

nymphs straddling their own wet skins and sleeping

asterisms plunging planets into the tiny circularity

of heat the plangent syllable evoked just once before

the inevitable moment when the machines go off

and cease working their red lights and isn't that

how summers end and the nostalgia for combs and

the restless intuition to die at the right time and

the jazz solo in the dark corridor

11-23-21

THE BROTHER OF THE MISSING MONTH

the enhanced syllable of the missing month
overturns the vocalic hand of fate the solar
consonant doubled for its insomnia the edges
and the center confused in a circularity of
yearbook ritual the mental ephemera of light
boundless inactivity of stone and gravel to
assume roles of the *unknown* in a symbolism
that denies a past and the sudden and bright
wheel rerouting the sky's erratic evolution
acceptance and denial at once of the centrifuge
and its metaphor of smokeless fire the isotope
and the poetry of no beginnings like planets
born tomorrow headless amok in the western
hemisphere of perpetuity and am I alone a copy
of the *other* shattered in a reflection of still
another in an imitation of pronoun and mask
dancing in the orangery of historical repetition
a vast but insignificant portion of space allotted
to the frame of reference which is the brother
born in the prophetic zygote tender elusive
as grass waiting for its borders to increase come
nightfall and the small predatory insects whose
blazing eyes drill through pyramid and song alike
a luster to recall whole days together ruminating

perambulating the interstices between logic
and unreason the outer atmospheres of childhood
slopes and lawns and tree-roots like maps of cities
that only exist underground radio signals that
announce the end of all futures the ennui and
riverbank of time's erroneous direction rumor of
salvations rebirths transmogrifications *Buddhas*
made entirely of liana and chalkstone & numbers
no sooner counted than erased by great invisibility
it is where to stop that we cannot know to ken
the smaller intentions of lunar divagations
the length of sorrow on summer evenings the noise
the gods make when they can sleep no more and
the pitch and sulfur of human thought a precipice
that has no other shape but the missing month
and for this we write and alone into the night

11-25-21

KAZANTZAKIS : AN EPIPHANY

dawn the early Greek resin of pines
small suns glinting higher than thought
racing entelechy to its tomb smothered
in dew dandelions frescos painted on temple

walls Apollo versus Daphne of fleet foot
the heroes chased by that ogre death on
their shields capsized from steeds sleeker
more swart than the sky's invisible horses
of metal shining brassy hot the breathing
of gods in tempests of flare and height
so doom-spun the days revolve from a
single spark of insistence and envy airs
incandescent and wild a book no page
can hold the words literally a few sounds
denatured with images flying athwart
the glassy distances of holy seas foaming
to take the rapture of the minute polished
as the skins of nymphs perched on moving
rocks myth and metaphor the great and
stuttering winds wrapped around a single
vowel the statue of speech ! how raised
arms the augur flings a blind cast of lamps
shaking as earth does in its terrific gyre
and in silence heads lowered darkness
them takes in a swift curtailment of wings

11-25-21

FROM A VEDIC DISTANCE:
AN EPITAPH

playing tag through space and time I lost

track and trace fleeting as it was of his shadow

narrows between the moon's curbstone and

the sun's obligation to leaf and grass a river

was nearby and the myths of ears and dragonflies

dipping the body into the great error of memory

elaborate as an ant-hill asleep and what of ancient

hands and the garage where darkness is born and

the painted rocks meant to signal passing clouds

rumor of atmospheres that scour the legend of speech

the encomia and threnody of all that has ever been

a lens that magnifies water and its drowsy planets

where would the head dwell ? even as his silhouette

passed like a scourge into a waiting room full of

satyrs with eyes like cubicles of lust and envy

down he went ! a smattering of postcards sent

from a Homeric mausoleum depicting the Descent

the quicksilver moment when the mind trades

its archaic gear for the Unknown passage

nothing but the remnants of a voice whispering

through Tuesday's labyrinthine telephone

nothing but the ensuing deconstructed silence

José Argüelles, RIP, Mar 23, 2011

11-26-21

HYMN TO THE GODS WHO ARE ONLY RIDDLES

deities of frogs and mice who bring rains

and devastations and alter islands in their course !

deities of splendid Moghul thrones and dice

who are deaf and live on opium and perfumes !

deities of the honorific pronoun and false promises

whose aerial archaeology and ladders lead nowhere !

I am in prayer wheel of redundant consonant *Sigma*

invoking the sun of ire and pretension lauding

the ever graceful *apsarases* for their wistful distances

I am in sand and retribution somewhere near

the seventy mouths of the holiest waters

and with hands not my own shape entryways

to sleep and the transmogrified syllables of wind

when did I ever believe ? was there a future

laid out on the sacrificial altars the lowing of cows

the granulated effect of ink scattered across the page ?

priests of sanctified saxophones and trade-unions

whose intercession brings the world closer to the gods !

repeat and keep repeating the aphasic mantra !

I am at once here and not here a nebulous entity

a mask wandering in the pits of language and business

a foreigner in my own skin a twin without a double

copying and erasing with black-eyeliner the schemes

and duplicities of glass-blowers and presidential candidates

hear me out *Invisible Ones* ! I cannot remember your names

correctly I am a convex mirror reflecting motors

that traffic in sound engineering and death by diesel

earth is on its way out ! millennial droughts

mutations of mutations of cell biology gone wrong

students hacking secrets of outer space and selling

forged souls of Doktor Faustus to those who deal

in illicit chocolate and gold trade and there are doors

and windows sealed by the Pharaohs who feared more

than anything growing tiny and disposable and

there are units of speech only statues can hear and

oratorios built upon myths of Adonis and Osiris

and I double back and forth over the Map and listen

for the intense whiz of Diana's chaste but murderous darts

but hear only the voluble passage of time through

the mercurial eye of the Minotaur slain by a red thread

deities of insect motivation and screens of fireflies

whose immemorial births never took place !

deities of sepulchral shape and looming smoke lanterns

who exist only in the falsified futures of light-years !

me ! gone ! prayers for the day that will never come

for the child stolen by the x-ray for the memory

of a week innocent of ambulance or siren

deities ! pornographers of the triplicate heavens !

absences ! mine are the leaf and grass and stone

where the head prepares itself for eternal silence

SHANTI SHANTI SHANTI

11-27-21

A FUNERAL TEXT

redundant with echoes that lack origin and sounds

the text of entry and recall reverberations of mortality

a child a man a fragile entity an emphatic and what

consider the missing parts the disunion and dissonance

gold and attributes of darkness single and multiple

the oceans rising to their knees and clouds racing

to the theater where geminated consonants combine

with the ruddy elements triplicate spheres that hover

density of sleep the unremembered component of thought

such and the other in the wings always a fossil trilobite

something to linger over longing for distances far to

the right of the hills and dialects spun out of discarded

vowels the statuary of memory each his own way going

towards a place called home the darkened second floor

the munitions in the basement the hobbled stairway

plunge down like planets out of orbit symbol and metaphor

the willingness to pursue chasing the more obscure noises

reading the lips of seers in their vedic trance rumor

and sabotage of meaning the lunatic mind backwards

filing disturbances of cognition in the wrong bin and

stepping over enigmatic pools reflecting basins meres

the tombs ! the morgue repeated Thursdays and dawn

never to manifest again its roseate and swart destinies

hoof and wheel the circularities of time ! poetry and

stasis the signals of oblivion moving grasses and gravel

the resting place of the soul identified as circumferential

sculpted deities five thousand eight climbing in Madurai

language in stone syllables that take centuries and high

to the beyond of the eye galaxies of pure intransigence

and in the end nothing more than hospital sheets

wrung out to dry on a tenuous repercussion of smoke

what is immortality but the formation of the *unseen* ?

and *who* props up the six spaces lest all totter and fall ?

11-29-21

MI SUEÑO DE RITA MORENO

para Armando Rendón

the emptiness the sheer emptiness and superfluity

of this infernal cocktail party not the ennui of TS Eliot

but the cosmic gathering all such affairs past midnight

must be commingling and conjugating space and time

the dead the living-dead zombies and immortal rejects

jostling for a terrestrial footing for a nibble of the prize

sallow-complexioned fixed stares but loud with rumble

and gossip of noiseless chatter the defiant lamps and

stubble of strobe-lights dancing wildly samba and rumba

all manner of foothill dialects out of proportion sizes

of both ink and stencil and it's always two AM lucid
hour when dreams can only come alive under watch
of San Juan de la Cruz and picking you Armando out
of the rout and riot I choose to be my Vergil to guide
though this mélange and farrago the strange pallor
and peace of your countenance across the eons by
the elbow you take me to cruise through galaxies of
bad literature and even worse movies suddenly to my
far left lying on her side on a ratty couch and clad
in a cheap tight flimsy red dress is Rita Moreno not
a Bollywood Natalie Wood doppelganger projection
but the real thing body and soul black shellac eyes
purposefully both strikingly beautiful and mournful
"I'm a Spic" she declares laughing as if she were on
a Sixty Minutes interview and fawning the air with her
penetrating gaze just come down from the Hills and
at once there is nothing else despite the rise in volume
of sound and serious discussion of trade unions and
developing peoples on the southern rim and the echolalia
of the Fathers in their tombs of distance and longing
and the sad thing is she just wants to borrow money
from me a poet, Armando, and I recall besides *Spic*
other terms *Wetback* or just *Dirty Mexican* and rumor
of plate glass reflections in American outback and poor
chevvies and rattle-trap Fords and roads of misery
to borrow a thousand dollars from me she laughs showing

the extent of her dazzling teeth and of course I can
do that I can even use my credit card just as the din
and fracture of the atmospheres begin to dissolve
the report of this vision this mutilated copy of events
that never happened song and dance of the faceless
for whom a Motel-Six is the last refuge and when
I turn to look again the couch is bare only the worn
red dress flung lazily in despair remains of my dream
the universe born in the error of a missing hemisphere !

11-30-21

MUCH CLAMOR AND SHOUTING

and art thou like-minded to step in between
mortals and gods putting an end to the fray ?
the dilemma exists not in stone but in language
I was high-heaven minded going about my text
revising quotes of air and wind sandstorm and
technically speaking the baleful waters when
what Ho a cry from the Stygian boatman
was I next ? head to rock soundless noises
stolen from the city-destroying goddesses
I was in plenty disarray and which way to
go blocked the passage of syllable and augury
flexions of irregularity and a symbol shining

in the back brain to wit the confusion grown

swart and big the hoof and tramp of horses

somewhere outside my ear and shot hearing

through the wood a tangle of mistaken steps

worked the one vowel that carries ascension

could there be a joy to waking things and mark

a finish to the road if I could learning meant

nothing a walk to the library minutes from

the entry to the clinic of memory the underground

path to cognition and sighting across the stream

a blaze of pyres and silence the color of metal

reflections of a brain untoward and to wrestle

with the commands and set the lines straight

deliver me from the parallel life ! it was a single

notation in the unheard music night-spell

dangerous lessons recited unconscious dark

the writing unraveling in its clay bed wedges

squiggles interpretations of bird-cries bright

and flush with an oriental system of quarrying

using a finger dipped in red ink and chaste

with promises to never again call upon *Powers*

of the other side did I then swoon striking

the dead-level substratum of sleep a pronoun

lost forever in the swirling yellow cloud-masses

script and breath the one divided from the other

as if to live were a matter of reading leaves

and the immense array of twilight grasses

12-01-21

A QUARTET : THE BLEEDING PHOTOGRAPH

i

how is it far from the opposite the end has no

sight illusory structures of air lasting a minute's

notice or less are we moving at the length of our

shouts the time it takes to travel in memory to

the first pronoun of skin the sun's immense cataract

a summer is gone before and the houses standing

once in the middle now asleep on the depths of lawn

almost a consonant in width the frame and suffering

each has a hand in sorrow no mitigation and swarms

the ear with entelechy of the hive a section turning

sulfur-yellow dominant as sound is possible given

the interim between one death and the following

so much for feeling and the asterisks crowning

the heights just after the implosion sky-rocketing

clouds of theater and anguish the lingering leaves

by the tip of the yard and the flux of motor-oil

seeping under the foot-mat a fiction of entries

when the last was never verified unseen and lost

ii

repetitions on corrugated surface as twilight dives

eleven into night equidistant from the norm and its

hemispheres when can we tell if the world is going

to end or the child will come back broken afternoons

when the sun's homophone remains fixed in the ceiling
or the doctors sawing and humming in their white
disasters passing for robes the plenty of a substantive
derailed inactivity linking planet to the unbound far
to the west of the ridge where dialects are born what
that crying is if it originates in the undetected wound
afterwards the coma and the verbal infix and the plot
to surrender the floor how it turns into Friday darker
than the previous and asking the wall-clock the hour
stopping as it does for a reflection even as traffic
speeding from an equation for breadth absolves
nothing frightening because it cannot be discovered
the longing for doors and dreaming in grassy warmth
head split by the remotest month now unremembered

iii

the bleeding photograph we don't know anybody's name
they are standing in rows of three for a schoolyard echo
fade and pensive their gazes gnarl in the latent sunlight
aslant and thrust into the core central to the group a
lack of distinctiveness or the perjury of dust settling
on the celluloid figures or they are sutures smiling
into the vast penury of air each of them is the many
who are gone for whom grammar is memory not
words which are inconstant nor the noise of sleep
redundant in peripheries where time loses weight

gravity being the principle of grief the unending as
written by bards of inconsequence but in latitudes
unbeknownst to them atmospheres form and rains
of lassitude a longing will not still against windows
that look out to southern vistas where the dead
coalesce in shapes of six or eight a repercussion and
extent of deities hovering like hummingbirds in
search of ink and hues the dimensions are great
the futilities and the unwillingness to let go

iv

as mortals are but gamblers housed in bad linguistic
structures the darkening rout and semblances to night
sister of oblivion the galaxies portend nothing other
than the immaterial substance that gave them birth
an error in routing and depths never uniform we are
yielding to the indelible Unknown and fractured
by the light that kindles stress the accent that comes
just before the accident the plural of water rising
to take first the knees than the hips of consciousness
an elevator and a box tied with red string and a bit
of music from the junior high orchestra oval and
caryatid the famous remnants of the archaic as
pulverized stars coming back to haunt and the hills
that grieve utmost as hymns memorized in sleep
of creation the vowel and fled in weeping asterisks

legends of planet Gaia what of the others a rumor

only of their existence and battle stanzas and gods

plying a loom somewhere in the outback of space

12-02-21

THE VEDIC GOD *YAMA*

and who is the boy driving the chariot
without wheels so young was he ever born ?
in all of space is there one so bright and swift ?
soundless the origins of creation and suddenly
the great Noise and the reverberation of metals
and the unfurling of immense cloud masses
ruddy echoes and powerful gusts of porphyry
is there a god amongst this turbulence of hues and
distance one that directs the height of the waters
or extends the various structures of air and winds
across the domains of the inchoate and shapeless ?
hands come into being that hold the reins
and steeds alert to the color black and perspiration
and hooves that clatter on the backs of time
from the inert arise the vegetations and dialects
the distinctions of light and gravity the famous errors
of birth and sleep and from a small pink shell
come into being hearing and sight and doubt

but the boy ! he is *death* the only mortal !
understanding is not in his purview nor the intellect
to apprehend language nor the various integers
that blossom into flowers with their hosts of bees
without origin he is ageless driving his vehicle
recklessly between the planets of adolescence
and alcohol and there is much smoke and vehemence
to pronounce correctly what has never been uttered
poles are erected at either end of the spectrum
and galaxies that have learned to swirl and burn
themselves out of existence and the thought of immortality
the rock and the chasm and anatomies of gas
how did so many attributes come into being ?
and what of *us* the shadows that motivate mirrors
or who excel in the use of pronoun and mask ?
is it death the makes the sun's homophone to shine ?
tender are the years on earth the redundancies of act
the repercussion and hallucination of memory
all that come to grief and end in the houses
that exist on the southern rim far from human ken
there where the boy wheels his yellow-gold chariot
to disappear into a second or third infinity

12-03-21

THE PERFORMANCE

the charioteer speaks perfect Sanskrit!
yet have we wasted our lives on words
which is the loudest consonant and
which is the longest vowel ere we enter
the deer park and avoid the tracks of smoke
and ire and to whom address these strophes
to which of the deities of the unseen realms
offer prayers of phonetic decay and noise
players in stagecraft error and rumor
stuttering and plague of statues the height
of longing and heat noontimes and silence
was love ever so inarticulate? can never
mean what we say and extend hands into
scripts of air and emboldened by emotion
break forth into rhyme and song fools
that we are with cigarettes and stairways
the escape valves marked *peligro* in red
phone calls to numinous lovers whose
existence hangs by a frayed thread copies
of imagined dead who linger in the vestibule
unable to talk and direct sounds into the
great plenty of the atmospheres where
diatribe and speculation imitate mortal
misgivings the entire experience of breath
gift and anatomy of the *unspeakable*
"I am over it" and stumbles off stage

into the arms of the puppeteer whose
incorrect grammar and fumbling strings
lack distinction pure hill dialect and loss
twilight of the gods they call it down
there among the grieving rocks and
gravel pylons tottering towards the sky
inches and thumbs of mental tempest
seas that gather their knees in despair
the guardian angels as such are trash
cities like onion skin built one upon
the other in sequences of ten and three
archaeology of water and shadows
bone-structure of the earliest texts
dissolution and desire embracing lyrics
interjected between nostalgic tropes
chivalry and dolce stil novo astride
the sun's uncontrollable mounts swart
and heaving through galactic comedies
a day and then no more ! poetry !

12-04-21

THE UNDETECTED WOUND

for Tom Farber

what it's all about death and dying

fictions of thought and matter opposite

poles unfelt and beyond sound the note

unheard merging into coffin-colored clouds

a planet at a time going out like lamps expelled

to farthest corners of space outside of time

junction of heat and gravity the sleeping mind's

untraced depths before waking to dawn's

brightest rubies adorning her left hand

that takes night by her jet-black masses

of hair bejeweled with galactic antimatter

flinging the shapeless beauty to the antipodes

where windows frame the lost solar syllable

blackening like tapers in Spain's fierce bedlam

down the road past the mountain buried

in its honorific pronoun the splendor we

assembled to cast our lots and mourn the one

gone wrong in lesions of an undeclared

heart the long forgotten wound with its loud

and wild synthesis of circumflex and doubt

what it's all about death and dying

resin and tar capsize insane waning cities

and shadows across summer's cornfield rows

lovemaking in soil and sweat are slashed

by light's crippled metal emerging from

a southern hemisphere with words of no

known tongue that anoint the evening leaves

with silently bleeding persons whom the Muses

have inspired to write in lunations of ink

of suburban disappearances that occur

in the hieratic hiatus that shifts through dark

and unexpressed marble looming inches above

earth's now forsaken surface the sorrowing

as inexplicable as heaven's raging asterisks

12-05-21

FLOWER-THIEF

buzz word of Sanskrit playwright

black and yellow bumble bee you

alight on Shakuntala's roseate face

adoring her mimicry of fright her

hands put you to flight to trace

aerial syllabaries in the Dravidian sun

a blaze of unspoken heat a noon borrowed

from eternity and placed neatly between

dialects of salt and ivy the corrupted

sounds and embellished rules of thought

the lessons of touch and loss blossoms

with petals of infinite jasmine fragrance

mendicants stop to stare with drunken eyes

the maid with her sweet accomplices

so far from palace rites a honeyed

interjection and vowels loosed without end

consonants are gone ! the world itself

is the emblem of absences beyond delight

foot-step in coral and ambiguity as if

the ruddy god whose feathers turn to flame

were about to descend and adorn her hair

twice and thrice small shouts of glee

the darkened meters that underscore

love's awful triumph with unseen glances

from shadows anxious to talk again

yet does the flower-thief whiz and burn

in the poetic circle of smothered air

come ! they dance and imitate masks

encrusted with stolen jewels and sing !

when will the king himself appear ?

12-05-21

THESEUS

whose eyes will the god of love beset ?

what pilgrim of the heart foisted by trials

of rock and gravel on the way to *Elysium*

will sauntering falter and into the dark pool fall ?

what was first will never be again the poem

and rite of heat and tribulation the fast glance

into the beyond when death survives another life

the dialect by the many spurned the tender

unbearable sense of never regaining balance

'twas love on whose promontory poised I stood

prepared to fall forever into its abyss and words

all failed and sounds like leaves in their lunacy

to speak when darkness pulls up its knees

and hails the moon most perishable of the Muses

does ancient literature too collapse in anachronistic

shreds and rags the tattle-ends of inflexions

noble for their incompletion and breath

the waning suffix the vain effort to proceed

into the maze of winnowing air the subterfuge

and consonant of earthly delusion and hands

that tell no tales but the one of eternal loss

that fold and unfold grasping for knowledge

of the sun's destructive homophone and alas !

then am I in surfeit of ignorance a victim

of memory's corrupted syllables the loud and pale

an instant in an eternity reflected in passing glass

mirror edge and symposium of laughing girls

adolescence spent in a single day the secret

of light and bodies abandoned in the casual ditch

by the roadside where multiples of Trojan Hector

appeal to shades that seem to shake with irreverence

but only the bruited noise of gods and mountains

gives off hints of another time a world

of forgotten alphabets and betrothed entities

who have been denied the wings to fly

and I in the mist and fogs of philology begin again

to learn the simple lesson that love has no language

and to live in the motel of illusions is man's

labyrinthine lot until sleep takes its toll

for Ariadne did I deceive

12-06-21

THE ORESTEIA

did go no further than when I was young

a language half-spoken talking to sleepers

in their wake a function of adolescence

to assume everything and watch the diesels

roar down the pike hauling below their wheels

the Greek kids who had strayed into the fray

the wrong way at a bad time when the restaurants

of the holy fathers were shut and the weekends

louder than when I was taught but not to think

to ascend the vowels of some divine discourse

holding a book of terms to the left and eye

high and fixed again to fall and threads of

narrative snapped in the middle who ever knew

how it would end the hero and his lust the spears

and greaves the flimsy metal buckling a goddess

had no problem wreaking vengeance on

the huddled pronouns caught in the vestry

awaiting doubt to strike dumb the last of

the first to cruise in sun-stroked belvederes

a wonder to this day memory has any currency

is it for sorrow we learn to write or plagiarize ?

thumbs of time and legend and still the mountain

holds its own in patristic measures all hollow

in the middle where we are supposed to quarry

the mind for new dimensions *I am Orestes !*

trilogies of stagecraft and plight the megacycles

of sky with its oriental clouds and fission

a thunderbolt is a theater with dressing and Boom

vagaries of cosmetics and the drenched body

found listing at the gate waiting for night to open

its back screen portal and what of the cyclopean walls

just outside the text with its gold assonance and

heights and pointers to the traveling asterisks

of galaxies forbidding shades of *Klytemnestra*

in her bathrobe and blood sizzling in the miasma

weather of misfortunes the babbling masks

screwed on to fit forever and all fall down the coats

and pantaloons torn at the helm and ahoy the ships

sighted in their troubling bay the sails blackened

by the sun's terrible hypothetical syllable

shifts of months over a single day and cocktails

at five in the department's fire-escape

who will respond if the phone rings and no one

is there just the enormous hiatus between breath

and its double the bottled music of the *Furies* ?

12-07-21

THE SACRED GRASS

what was our life but a brief stroll

in the Vedanta Park a warm afternoon

somewhere between aching and grief

the spotted deer tiny in their horizon

of vanishing shrubbery and waning light

ignoring where west is nor that east had
lost its border and above in a mottled sky
scudding cloud-wefts seemed to spell
the oncoming attrition of the heavens
how did the grass learn to end ?
fortune was on the side of the gravel
that formed a driveway though no
vehicles were visible but for the silent
roar of a sun-driven chariot up above
and the house darkened by too many
summers with windows blind to the day
and bookcases with mysterious tomes
and pamphlets about the passing life
or the death to be pronounced in dense
intricate sermons of avatars and saints
too many to be alphabetized and dim
blurred photos of the soul in its plural
manifestation a surfeit of shadow ready
to elevate into the secret shutters of
the second floor where rows of beds
centuries waiting for inhabitants who
will never get past the stairway before
evolving into entities of smoke and haze

12-07-21

THE UNBRIDLED MARY LOU OF THE MIND

rich in behavior her hair the wedlock of a god

promised to another and not revived of spirit

the throne of illusions so many the unbridled

mind in the various motels of south Broadway

could only dream that it existed once and looked

askance at the burning taper with its paper signature

could only weep head bowed to the Master of Destiny

the floor boards like the empty cupboard objects

bereft of any symbolism the coherence of memory

a questionable dialect with its unassigned hills

which only while sleeping can be attained a version

of the *Popol Vuh* in metal and transcript on verso

the text a hegemony of unrelated details hacking

through jungles of liana grass towards an oblivion

in Spanish only the frayed and until now unnoticed

the way she wore her sweater and pinafore in winter

back against the automobile hood and panting in

a luxury of homophones meant to give heat and hints

of what lay beneath the woven and knit landscape

could I but recall with any dignity the ribbons and

combs the large safety pin the embroidery of bees

at the dance spellbound in ethereal silence embraced

to a pronoun of no sizable dimension the weight of

a feather on the Egyptian scales against the soul

a loss forever the grimoire of cries shouts and depths

turned the page over beneath the dormant lid to

read an inscription dated January 1954 ! a fission

of confused lunar dates months collapsed into one

isolated moment beneath the beta sun of adolescence

the many skins and the language of snakes loud

in proportion to the origins of poetry a given moment

when the hiatus bursts red and the personae swarm

looking for the appropriate century and the twin

from whom poetry and augury arise as an accident

in the vacant courtyard finds the self attenuated

a barely visible shadow something indistinct with

chrome and lipstick and a drug of powders riding

the skull towards its own occidental demise the fell

trance of breath multiplying a simple vowel into

clouds beautiful as a triptych in helium and mercury

BANG ! the various entities scatter in as many deaths

as the consonant *MU* can allow in the instant when

eternity revolves its wheel back into the silent leaves

that adorn the distant brow of her of summers born

and laid to rest in some November cornfield pure

and anonymous

12-08-21

THE RANSACKED ILLUSION

O mundo não é humano—Clarice Lispector

no horizons an unlit sun and deaths multiple

as the unmovable digit five floors below earth's

surface where madness and the entelechy of light

embrace as dreams that squander men's minds

a lasting wound a sore that does not cease running

implore the gods for one day less ! push back

the margins of ink the soundless emphasis of sky

retire from the noise and verbiage of statues in

their noontime dialogue with immortality

what matter the undressed lace of the lunar

syllabary mouthing the hushed forever of grass

and stone the here and now of imbalanced thought

an edge to brain unraveling in dichotomies of sand

the plagiarized vow to never again and fists raised

to harbor rains cloud-work of unstitched planets

plunging from the eye's highest lamp to circulate

in false histories of nymph and asphodel or sleep

in crematoria of burnt asterisks the spatial *dot* !

what is it to become a photograph recording device

of deities disguised as clods of dirt or fish-bones

errors of spite or envy rumors of Olympian ire

wars ! the distinctions between heart and tongue

corrosions of minor mental states the smaller deer

that nibble on the margins of time falling drugged

into streams that carry love-songs and amphetamines

into other dimensions worlds tinier than an eyelash

and still a-swirl in the province of Gog and Magog

this is the last of many copies of a poem without

beginning a meaningless direction a southland

occupied by the final thoughts of betrayed lovers

ransacked illusions ! a high-school yearbook effaced

by hands that have yet to be invented and you ask

dear reader , you ask , *why*

12-09-21

UNWRITTEN STROPHES

walking back through space across the top of time
souls of flower-spirits now long gone mingle with
my dead ! I drive around detours
up ungraded roads through bramble paths
the daily routine of careless existence
subtracting days from an imaginary calendar
the fatal lesson of an unachieved grammar
the misinterpreted rules the phonemic disorder
words out of line with their sounds buzz
and hum of the ear in the hive of sleep
creatures who have come and gone in a trice

their fabulous embodiments wrapped in vowels

of pure distance elementary and spacious

with hills where dialects converge and go lost

the undergrowth of sorrow always abiding

in a next room muffled and indistinct cries

sobbing between the knees grief at the shoulders

hemlines of wasted cloth and the dark matter

of the unsuspected wound the mind glued

to a photograph of what might have been

who was in the second row third from left smiling

for the brief instant of a shutter's eternity

click and resonance of longing the archaic flaws

dimensions of hues and absence of consonants

the dream of a different life counting the numbers

of breath allotted to the fated child whose

shadow without looking leaped into the void

alas ! the reflections never come back

simply the empty mirror and the repercussion

of wheels traveling on the far side of the mountain

mesmerized by yesterday's waning sun

memorizing syllable after syllable of unwritten

strophes dedicated to Adonis or Osiris

the very myths of water light and ether

boundless treachery of the unbidden cosmos

as it travels its reckless speeds into oblivion

12-10-21

MNEMONICS

how can it be everything is reduced to memory

less than paper thin or just puffs of air invisible

to the passing mirror that erases as soon as it

records the illusory figures who imagine the self

as a walking resonating pronoun the nerve and

ray the eye fixes projecting the mind's vast

picture of a world teeming with objects and matter

that instantaneously disappear sensation and

outline the shadows that go to sleep the hues and

distances that are corollaries to spatial dimensions

peninsulas of gas eroded islands suffixed to clouds

that vanish in the heat of noon mime and acrobat

of intelligence children embryonic images going

about the business of cheating and trifling as *adults*

death threats that pass as love letters and ciphers

clipped to vowels that hover intransigent above daily

traffic aspersions and mountains travelogues and tales

spun out of rumors derived from history's grievously

long and mendacious chronicles all the grandeur that

poses as victory trophies but wavering tissue of memory

mortals subtracted from their essences dead by the time

they leave the womb fossilized mechanics of thought

doors that open and close on the finger that searches

for its past in evening grasses the longing and breadth

of error infused in the personal drama all imagine

to be one's own secret the plethora and diminishment

of mind ! fast-track to nowhere in the maze of three

trillion galaxies unidentified and without individuality

memory suffocating in punctuation and phonetic disorder

death-bed of dreams x-ray of doubts and suspicions

that nothing ever really happened but in the sad

and labyrinthine receptacle of illusions echoing

between yesterday and the day before yesterday

tombstones erected in the death before birth

I remember sitting in the movies with you my arm

around your shoulders and the fragrance of your hair

12-11-21

THE ARCHAEOLOGY OF SOUND
para nuestra hermana Laurita

dear brother I am writing you this letter

from a place nowhere on the map somewhere

between the latitudes of breath and the longitudes

of memory the streets have no discipline and the

hills same as ever have just changed dialect and

wonder why and how what disease transmitted

itself to you without my knowledge pirate and

traveler down under and although three hundred

sixty five days a year make it is just minutes
since your voice last imitated my voice in a resonance
that brought the oceans to their knees and planets
we only saw by day fulminated exploded burst into
orange and brighter than noon flames and died
just as you did still I don't get it why it happened
the way it did not as when we lay on our backs and
guessed which of the summer galaxies was ours
only the immense grass and the encircling bushes
of the back yard and the willow and plum trees
and the often taken hikes to the banks of the Zumbro
not to speak of the library with its mysterious corridors
that led all the way to Yucatan or the fourth dimension
or the pom-poms and celebrating girls on Friday nights
watching games that little interested us the foreigners
who ambled up and down the numbered avenues
of that wretched Minnesota town wondering why
and trying to figure out when we would die which
of us would be first and what music would be playing
looking at the movie theater marquees for secret
warning signals assuming the repeated canyons
Randolph Scott would round on his mechanical mount
and the bridge from which we stared down at
the Heraclitean flux and Wow the first rush of alcohol
all written in a book that had no start and the funerals
of enigma and scout the trees that obeyed a secret
alphabet and the archaeology of sound which

we pocketed with our cap-pistols bang bang watching

the linen of the clouds scud past whatever the eye

could not reach but really I don't understand why

I am still here listening to the radiators buzz and hum

their winter code and message and you forlorn in some

urn or just a handful of cinders redundant with

silence do I cry do I waste my time recalling snowfall

and leaves changing hue like colors radiating from a wheel

that goes to sleep and side by side in an infernal joy

of learning there was no *other* just the simple and

extravagant soul we shared ever since some obscure

hour of night in watery Tenochtitlan four hundred eons

before the passing of sound into noise and finding

our selves suddenly awake near a clothesline where granny

set the clothes out to freeze into stiff copies of personas

remember how we listened to the mourning doves

telling ourselves they were messengers from the paradise

we had just lost

we had just lost

and cannot finish this missive this bric-a-brac of syllables

these loan words from some dark *Sprachbund* far

below the equatorial dissent of memory

that comic book world we inhabited

pretending

12-12-21

WHAT IS LITERATURE

no end and no beginning so the song goes

reaching into the space where memory

blurs fades pales a shadow-play of silhouettes

noise and error reverberating in echo-chamber

and stone and grass and clinging leaves and

the long evenings when no one comes home and

yearning for a moment for the perfection

that only comes with eternity a distance so

far to the right of the window that looks out

to the vast and archaic panoply of the stars

turning green a dazzle of rumor and imperfection

we lay claim to nothing the doors shut of themselves

footsteps and cigarette smoke and the strange

illusion that we are suspended in existence

that somehow sleeping will make it better

augment and superfluity of sensation passing

from the planet where speech originates to

the planet riddled by aphasia and amnesia

will the day ever come ? roads wake the sun

fields glistening with the novelty of dew

and rows of fragmented sounds snippets of words

rattle and junk in the ear filled with half-truths

lies legends mythic assertion of deities and demons

we rotate the sky revolving it somewhat to the right

a hand takes into account the mission of bees

collecting what it can of the plethoric hum

and buzz the hive which is a mountain and

below it the ridges and furrows of dialects and

fractions of citadel cyclopean walls jiggered

and uneven in scope and destiny and a spear no less

leg-fittings of alloy and the measure of broken statues

caught in a lingering dream of cities and fire

is it enough to announce our direction ?

we rise and stretch our newly formed bodies

and down the stairs and out the back screen door

into the open months of summer in search

of names ! the world is a vast lawn at times opaque

at others a formation of water and shouts of glee

or the joy of conquest in the spurious inch of air

that knots itself and turns to syllables elegiac

or oracular many times over and trees bidden

to perform the act of memory and mysterious

voices which are the rustling leaves of childhood

and to lay the head on the perfected stone and

begin to imagine this has happened before

chronicles and fictions known as history with

repercussions of death and tragedy

will we ever really understand ?

12-13-21

MEDITATION AT THE CREMATORIUM

the lights are all flickering and the rains

have written an ephemeral discourse on the glass

and what's of life left the leaves spent and tossed

into gutters where memory strains to hold back doubt

the curse of the heart ! call out as much as one wants

to have back the immutable shape of love in

its many countenances and mind's fragile effort

to stay some course ere the stars falsify their routine

and abandon the heavens tonight *the great outcry* !

the season's dull chill and dusk make ever more infirm

the belief that we have truly lived some few moments

of certainty the apparently squandered light and pain

the clinging shadows the sobbing in the eaves

in those moments awaiting the recourse of distance

houses of uninterrupted solitude and alleyways

the error of street names and school-day faces

reciting lessons from a grammar of augury rife

with the plenitude of dark-matter and the enormous

sounds after the storm of swollen waters and ever darker

depths to which the soul descends recognizing

nothing of the patterns and disorientations of sleep

the knee beside a cathedral imperceptibly shaking

the x-ray and nail-file that render memory useless

come back to me ! whatever thing it was that fit

the disposable coffin and the gorgeous trailing wreath

monumental incisions in air and winds blown out of a bottle

held in some deity's left hand the course of mountains

rivers that have nowhere to go winged echelons

of tawny demons hungry to eat the remains of evening

altars toppled sacrificial fires dimmed nothing but

the abandoned stairway to the third level and

phantoms passionately smoking cigarettes

somewhere near the top where threnodies accumulate

paper flowers broken funerary urns photographs

of heat on the island of Crete and ruin and desolation

of human thought after the concussion and accident

metal spent spinning into the detritus of space

what and how will *it* ever be remembered ?

12-14-21

THE AFFLICTION OF SOLITUDE

repetition of hours prose texts jumping

from the moon into the duality of sleep and waking

summon the dead from their larval dream of light

has been was and never will be again surfeit

of grammar and reason partition of space

into the famous bipartite elements of being

and dark matter such as it is today alone *out there*

insertions of memory merry-go-round of wooden horses

the kids a glee of laughter and an unbidden humor

of departure never to be seen again lost

in the amphorae and decals of an unearthed

archaic torso and to stare into its streaked oblivion

heat and the muscle of the sun's apparent homophone

only the streets do not return as they were

a rippling mirage of summer tarpaulin and splash

ingenuous harmonies of the untrained ear

and sudden and unreflecting gone ! empire of solitude

brick-paving and ivy trellis and the drooping shadows

cast by phantoms trying to return to this dimension

promises of sound the interruption of atmospheres

buzzing in the silence of heavens created by

words alone and the nonsense and error of poetry

drill and tone of emotions recitations by statues

on the parade near the court house where ghosts

declaim and argue for the existence of cities

in the warped routine of history if only to be read

and destroyed in the pre-fabricated afternoon of adolescence

when pronouns merge and defy the rules of mask

and to be left *alone* in the crowd suture and plinth

grief at the heart of what is experienced the total

anomie of love and despair *call me tomorrow*

wisps of perfumed hair and the longing to erase

footsteps and floral designs the winds that race

through the numbered avenues taking away the fragrances

vast invisibilities the mind creates dreaming

as one by one the planets fall from grace and isolated

on a rock lashed by evening tides the moon

in its guise of *nenuphar* disappears slowly in the sands

and treachery of distance a vanishing dot

in the perplex of time

12-15-21

BITTERSWEET

hearing the great word Hector entered

in the midst holding back the phalanxes :

God angels heavens elements plants

minerals animals man Paradise and Hell

thus the mirror that reflects the daily vision

loss and grieving every time the hand sets up

its alternate in a sleep of demons and

do rejoice ! a new day only to be shadowed

by memory of the multiple starts and stops

of the past in all its egregious and plundered

assertions the bodies laid to rest and burn

the holiest of moments is inspiration *and*

failure the inch of distance the slender
margin where insect and fossil gain on light
deathless entities swirling in a galactic fuse
nothing that can ever be named this life
the antipodes and sequence of deaths as if
anything can ever be counted and cataloged
breath alone ! listen with ears of stone the rain
that slackens in the labyrinthine winter dark
today ! the self sustaining promise to step
persisting in the mind's small snapshots
of intelligence and void the entelechy and
poetry love squanders in its sorrowing fate
do all things come to naught in a single instant ?
the terror of flame or flood that encroach
on human designs the shoe and comb and
small red music box the sound irreverent
of threnody and syllabary littered paradoxes
taken in the famous air's violent embrace
noises that chase the brain into its final round
and the *eye* that learns to read and behold
the sun in its brace of homophone and heat
wordless maze of eternal lamps that *blind !*
with what authors approach the twilight ?
elect Lope de Vega and Ariosto ! shepherd
and knight rocks and trees the very verses
that yield only silence in the end –

silver bows and vultures Father of the gods !

Minerva fallen from her hexameters of grace

and *Hector* slain and trodden in the dust

AOI

12-16-21

LISTENING TO BILLIE HOLIDAY AT 5 AM

what does it mean to dream of trees
souls trapped between the ligatures
of existence and non-being
           skeletal leafage
waving eerily in the boundless above
reminds of what and whom
did everything need to happen as it did ?
disbelief and mourning on the lawn
sun spots dereliction of duty hemispheres
long separated whirligig and asterisks
spinning out of control sleep and its other
the half of oblivion called yearning
alphabet of the heavens jazz and superstition
caravanserai of adolescent desires non-stop
phonograph records the dance of treachery

leaning out the window to touch the tops

of those two trees scraping against stucco

Chinese poetry ! plum and willow and

the small bridge arching the stream

where summer ripples between the banks

a hand idles in the current a face waiting

to die somewhere in the nearby cornfield

heat and evanescence human consciousness

more asleep than awake in the *wee hours*

reach down to the roots where memory

aching to remember the right moment

before the storm and darkness

I'll be looking at the moon

but I'll be seeing you

12-17-21

LA BREVEDAD DE LA VIDA

"Guárdate del animal hombre que tiene
el pensamiento en lo más escondido del corazón"

                Lope de Vega, Arcadia

the kingdom of France will have suffered and

all the ancient cities out to kill us since Sumer and Akkad

the stones that heat the chimes of history fly broken

in recorded airs and atmospheres now long vanished
in the ephemeral dust of thought with shame and scorn
do palaces like chimeras then glitter in the summer blaze
and we with the likes of popes and princes on our knees
pray to keep intact hip and shoulder ere we sleep
do distances then hover like mountains come to grief
and shades and phantoms with unremembered names
keep to our dreams the thin divide between breath
and the deathless south where are wont to wander
dazed the truly dead in whom we ourselves delve
searching for a language to interpret our aimless fate
what ! and dozens of pages into the soundless text
our minds a complex of watery tissue and lies about
grammar and the substance of daily discord and
the statues that sustain us in our false beliefs
come noon and the day's waste is too apparent
to museums and sprawling parks we lend our hands
stray and purposeless between cycles of renown and ire
then is evening with its fare of expense and debt
and night when all the leaves take in their silence
and the upper tiers of the heavens with starry cuneiform
which we fain would read and claim a drained victory
thus in a single day does our life measure itself
childhoods and winsome love affairs and sudden ills
the stricken body the phalanx of x-ray and disbelief
out with the last syllables of metaphysical rant
noise that proclaims parallel lives and sudden universes

the turning on a burning axle of the dying sun and
the phosphorous indignation of extinct galaxies
how little we have assayed to learn and does darkness
wrap around our legs and tumbles us in a sandy fray
alas and be gone *Literature !* pronouns fountains and
disguised shepherds with amnesia who roam the hills
lovesick with proportions of lunacy and reason
and like us have mistaken the road that leads within
and fallen drugged into arroyos the size of Spain
oak and mill-stone and sparkle of distant flares

12-18-21

BLIND-MAN'S BLUFF

the unfinished beast that from the wood comes
roaring with secret wounds heart-felt and stung
by unslaked desire we read him aright in texts
scrupulously memorized the god-head and fountains
trees that yield to human thought and leaves that bleed
with torment and night-spells that converge on pure
insanity do we keep reading and falters sight and
from the dense and swirling airs do catch a snatch
of talk perhaps in Spanish lingo and ominous clouds
the length of distance and yellowing masses the dense
and purposeless phase of learning to read new scripts
alphabets of chimera and trilobite to understand nothing

of the remaining text with other ears listen to the sound
descending from some unknown space in the heavens
to be witless like the stars that are trained to blink in
the darkest hours and bending to one another fail
to recognize those we loved so dearly and sorrowing
which emanates from some enchanted stone or the pulse
felt in the blowing heat around whose stalks winnow
emotions and longing for the ever lost we left unspoken
on some marble slab and the voices ushered in by
a slamming door and trails of spurious vowels that
sunder the head's tottering hemispheres and far
and wide the breach of meaning and noise and seas
that recollect the other day when placid pools and
gravel that linger on sleep's other side how tremendous
the felt incision of light the magnitude of the tragedy
wellsprings of cognition in foreign tongues and grasses
that lean against the errant song and yet for us to read
what cannot be written and the consonants and tones
of an archaic poesy strung between the planted coils
of memory what is that to us in our collapsed house
remembering cities built on escape routes of sand
the end of human worlds the tendentious claims of
property and domain how frail like the dandelion
at hour's end the puff of breath that diminishes the sky
and all lie down in blind-man's bluff alone to die
the game of school and growing up and grief

12-19-21

SELF-PORTRAIT DECEMBER 2021

the erased syllable of sleep lost forever

and what gives to memory its false inch

of secluded vision of eyelashes and wrists

the distance to the nearest mountain is

no closer than the moon or left to reading

in solitude the pages out of sequence and

numbers greater than three like a boomerang

come back to haunt the hand that shaped

from the gathering air a map of its own destiny

do I falter on the hemline that divides tomorrow

from its diagnosis and pushing forward no

small atmosphere cross over into the field

where summers parallel themselves and

heat drives its axis into some disordered past

I hear after the fact drowned voices and

the immense irregularities of dialect that

waver between the pool and its surrounding

hills the faded greenery the topless trees

scouring the skies for direction and complaint

this is no today but the unraveling of error

mother is locked in her photograph and

brother in his Aztec fourth dimension

there has never been a route leading south

nor the vagaries of an Olympian motel

riding on the outskirts of a temple ruin

and cities no greater than a thumbnail

governed by insect kings of total silence

have come and gone in the abyss of longing

a film unreels and pedestals of sound collapse

within the stone's virgin birth and grieving

befits holidays that fit no planet's hues

I am a pronoun in a text that needs a script

noise and junk of inhalation and remembrance

of the day that never was the saddest hour

the minute before anything ever happened

premonition of the end of space in details

that hazard meaning and vanish before

they can be discerned and all of this is me

the ancient accident of mask and knee

a previous fiction of cuneiform and death

whose dream has run its mirror and only

fragments of an unrecalled face stare back

from some profound lack of origins --

the starless and infinite night of time

12-20-21

BALLAD IN THE DEAD OF NIGHT

I saw the ship of memory go fleet past

my window pane and startled from a bed

that still was strange to me I rose and wept

all the summers occluded in a single blink

of an errant eye and cries that tossed into

the silent main of voices I scarce recalled

so much and so little in the flashing instant

when winds took shape unfurling tempest

and fevers and all that are dolorous to flesh

and soul alike I relinquished self and forwent

the archaic syllables that lament soundlessly

and from the bower of imprisoned thoughts

I tempted steps to take toward the orient

of despair and as the ship even farther swept

into a senseless and burning galaxy I felt

within me the many persons I had once been

pass from their husks and shells into the wake

left behind by memory's careening instability

ship and flower cloud and seamless sky heat

and grass that longs for fingers leaves that

yearn to speak and statues forever blind dumb-

founded in the pointless noon of another sphere

and hours added like sands to the revolving

wheel and worlds alone that could never be

I stood there shaking inside a book of glass

pages that of their own turned and decayed

as parchments withered in a blaze and words

that never once were heard came to my trembling

lips the orifice of insanity the threshold of some

mad deity who possessed & bound me to his vowel

as witless and enchanted I stared into the void

no trace of memory no lasting noise of time

12-21-21

THE OFFICE OF POET

beginning with the lower lip the procedure

of sounding the intimate noise from deeper down

the scales don't reach nor whether it is necessary

and sings alone the first of twenty two notes

promised to the Beloved on the eve of transparency

loud and single the simple lunar vowel the shape

of snow on a statue's hand the visible swiftly

become nowhere in sight for ages aching for

the upper lip to finish forming the elusive diphthong

whatever fixes the air with surprise of Bang !

and issuing from within the senseless accolade

the preach of love the divine obstacle of decay

translated from its medieval Pyrenean dialect

soundless avalanche and distich of memory come

to life like little flares that eyes open widening

on the scope of anti-matter the praise and lauds

holy thrice et cetera of the thing Unknown from

times of yore archaic stone the plunder of gravel

ceaseless swaying of the careers of grass where

no one but a goddess steps or may only holding

a nosegay of narcissi to eternalize the glance

the moment when the twain enter union beheld

and signed in dream-space the multiple entities

of air hovering glee and sorrow alike to share

and finally with open throat and hymning

all manner of unremembered tropes the verse

swiftly its own oblivion conceives and buries

inert the gift of words without meaning the high

and embracing drug that elevates and from

the roots of time ascends descends and disappears

12-21-21

ETERNAL FEMININE : WINTER SOLSTICE 2021

for Naomi Quiñonez

first the path of darkness the doors to nowhere

infernal glassware of the stars long dead in their crust

the lapse of eons and this tiny speck of dirt what can

it sustain breath and mountains chimes and obituaries
sorrowing pools and the distances between cities and
chronicles of uneventful reigns the depth and dearth
of the momentary exercised in empires and tsunamis
the length of childhood measured by a blade of grass
the totem beasts that govern dreams and solicitude
for the errant waters of sleep and waking what is
to find but others like us copies of ourselves pilgrims
draped shrouds and blindness to avert the possible
sensation that all has happened before yet this one day
the improbable composure of the sun's black homophone
self destructs night becomes all encompassing envelope
of distance and time only small luminous hands beseeching
another day to be a section of atmosphere designated
νοῦς and prayers to *Tonatzin Coyolxauqui Guadalupe*
if we are to know that origins do not exist and words
are the lapse of winds in the ear's tiny shell and cosmos
and derelict mortal are equally doomed from the start
fragile and tumultuous nonsense of mind the error
and adjunct to rumor playfield of imaginary deities
on our knees in gravel come the midnight hour and
spare voices from untranslated radios and the fierce
entelechy of animals in their winter dens creating
new universes that implode when the light hits and
Primavera with her trinities of sea air and comb is reborn
naked and fulsome thing shining like a nacre galaxy !
would we could understand the mysteries secret

raffle and lotto of misgiving and fate worried stone

abyss of yesterdays devoted to knowledge of trees and

speech of leaves and marble and the immense noon

of memory shattered forever by death the many deaths

we are to succumb ! shadows as ever lingering between

idiolect and cuneiform school days never outgrown

and lay the head between rock and rock this night

and become evanescent as the silent integers that

revolve forever unseen in the great lawn of space

12-22-21

THE DEATH OF ADONIS

the crocodile-bannered god of Love has wasted

his last arrows half-shot into the worldly miasma

into the fray and tumult into the very abyss of thought

fleeing mortals beasts half-human in appearance

lithe nymphs blossoming on lotus pools with harps

and combs and bracelet bejeweled arms that sing

nonsense into faint spring breezes somehow recalling

the ancient episode when rock and stone could

feel and did then anthems blow into coursing winds

and grasses bend to breath and bow as bodies

entranced sought each the other's silence and

crowns of light the fire from within did glow and loud

it was the archaic moment of union and reunion
of souls in that eternal revolution of unseen heat
wheel and iridescence of the atmospheres heights of
punctuation between dying stars and distances no
language could reveal yet how little has since transpired
how few have sensed the reeling dart that pierces
the heart's dark labyrinth and do we then wake to
lamps and registers of the hour and trade brief words
hands that have ceased to signify and watch as earth
collides with its former self and waters rise and tides
take cities one by one in the great year's failure to
overcome as the god of love himself eternal boy
suddenly aged gored by an invisible hunter's prey
and on the shores of Tripoli lays down his golden head
respiring one last time eyes clouded by some demonic
engine that purrs and crashes in the diminished space
where matter and time are reduced to unheard sound
and none are left to chronicle his life and fate
mourned alone by the deity Mother-of-Intransigence

12-23-21

GRANDMOTHER'S HOUSE ON FIRST STREET

for Laurita

however well it was explained to me
when it happened I didn't understand it
parts of the house remained forever dark
rooms without doors fireflies trapped in closets
stairs with nowhere to go but an unremembered sky
the end was always there the final breath the hand
losing grip of itself the shapes and shades
of an orient disguised as the promised future
the legends etched in cigarette smoke and words
dimly comprehended unraveling in the sleep
hidden in the basement beneath the paraffin lids
how much had to be discussed and pointed out
birth before death death before rebirth et cetera
there were glass book-cases with chalk dusters
and fuses that turned lights on and off but
I still didn't get it the annual transmogrification
the elicited prayers from the broken statue
they kept behind the kitchen the immense hours
of sheer emptiness on the front porch on the first day
of each passing month expecting the moon
would be drawn by incantation down to the well
where they kept extra faces in case of a misstep
all was error and rumor whispers between walls
and mysterious guests who appeared on holidays
for their share of the mystical feasts honoring

names no one could recall and everything so in place
yet so disjointed and the ennui especially of Sunday
afternoons when the dead returned to play Chinese checkers
the front yard was reserved for summers and
behind the house the small slope that led to
the entrance to Inferno beside the garage with its
whetstone and empty whiskey bottles and further
beyond the escapade of mosquitoes and heat
the garden plot tilled by Persephone every July
before being snatched away again by the Bogey Man
who otherwise dwelt in the attic where models
of missing airplanes hung wistfully from a timber
and secret voices cascaded out of futile dreams
about the next Fourth of July and the parade
and freedom for all who said their prayers
before going to sleep in beds of exile and despair

12-24-21

XMAS 2021

grammar didn't clarify which direction the season
nor whether hunting was out of the question
mountain and darkness both the common enemy
of thought there was no inkling and deeper still
the arroyos where mind tossed its sleep muddy and

obscure with presentiment dreams of archaic

stone formations eerie fragments of sky as if carved

glassware and dim reflections of those who had fallen

by the way either alcohol or a hidden sore a far

reach from the cloudless afternoons and sprawling

lawns with their museums of grass and ant-hill

could almost hear the cries the appeals for hands

to govern the small remains of their fate x-ray

and drug prescription and how could the holidays

ever be the same a remote sensing device lunacy

the extent of breath in its curtailed format of

broken promises and secret ridges and shelves

fuses and asterisks all the world slipping away under

the doormat sequences of high notes distant chorales

holy and soundless hymns that elude the dying ear

where was justice at the moment of birth ? alone

and with grief the sun rises over Bethlehem today

12-25-21

ONE DAY MORE ONE DAY LESS

even though rain sprouts from the asphalt

and angels scheduled for release next Thursday

must endure the morgue three more eternities

the street-cleaners have been canceled the debts

owed by students for accessing calculus and grief

it's all hazard a game of chance and breath

there never was an origin nor a spoken dialect

roaming somewhere in the hills just a Buddha-type

with hands of clay and eyes that couldn't open

unless upon command and the mendicants

with their little red carts and the osprey and

kestrel wheeling overhead and the seas that lack knees

and the hives of sudden memory with their swarms

of ancient bees with intellect and reason and compassion

and humans crippled with oriental pride and wives

basking in the glories of adultery and from nowhere

the end of time with its claxons and fire brigades

how often have we lived this life and asked

for one year less and winters with their neuter gender

and grammatical lapse of taste and to die alone again

in a bed separated from the sun's great ellipse

and hear the singing of the monochord the elusive

purpose of noise the brain fills with rankling and

dissent and morose and sorrowing entities begging

for an inch of shadow round the corner and disappear

taking with them the opportunities for oblivion

alone with the hundred units of sky and trapped

in the redundancies of the dream of youth and

the cornfields ripening and the heat in cycles

as archaic as Mycenae and verses of make-believe

that make one rethink the cyclotron and the dearth

of matter in the revolving silence that drains the ear

and to sleep again and to cease knowing anything

and dump the old soul into its broken engine

and pray the light will burn on the other side

12-26-21

THE DEERPARK AT SARNATH

"O inferno pelo qual eu passara—como te dizer?—
fora o inferno que vem do amor"
    Clarice Lispector, A Paixão Segundo G.H.

air is just a symbol a grace of forming winds talking

to grass the fundamental and even silent as the leaves

are at break of day depicted as remote reflections

in the eyes of the grazing deer and the pool of distance

darkening even as the sun's immense immobility seems

to hover over the theory of gravity and then do desires

spring as the illusion of knowledge turns green and

evanescent among those shadows apparently moving

through and around matter the concupiscent nucleus

of being human transient feeling apparatus of senses

it is not merely seeing but being able to see and the error

that entails becoming memory and the ear atonal and

dormant in the shell of memory culling from rumors
the noise that seems to signify and then curtains of
light fall and the expanse of lawn and shrubbery the trees
and clumps of growth as if waiting to listen to hear
receptacles of atmosphere and clouds suddenly looming
making a theater of the summer day coming to be
illusory as the playthings pretending to be other
than what they are copies of plasma and irritation
pronouns assigned at birth and recklessly wasted
in the event of another hour passing and then accidents
and the profusion of metal and misstep the diary
written in code and multiplied by an engine called
progress leaving the library behind in its sea of diagrams
and adolescence waking to a sequence of emotions
picture-book illustrations of performance and attitude
come then to this park to encounter not science but its ruins
the wreck of ideas like shattered cyclopean walls high
on the hills where dialects spawn schism and certainty
as if life were simply the ability to make a choice
without the responsibility for details and *learning* too
which is the great difficulty because it means *dying*
and there will come a moment when eternity's mirror
will encompass nothing and the masks and chisels once
considered necessary will be faint recollections and
instead moving one foot at a time through a narrow passage
called aging and returned in a dream to this park

to this finite disclosure of radiance and spectacle using

words however incapable they are of expressing tragedy

in its genuine format of loss and misplaced anger the wish

that things had happened otherwise and the immense sky

will seem boundlessly minor in its ever shifting azures

and to lay the head down on the rock smoothed by

tempests of invisibility and in that small sleep engender

fossils of recollection and innocence before proceeding

to the next phase of becoming awake and alert to

the surrounding hues and impermanence shedding from

the skin all notions of language and syntax even as sound

in its tremendous yearning for oblivion will define

for a brief hallucinatory instant the concept of a space

without origins and a fire indwelling will consume first

your *being* and then everything associated with it

burning deer grass trees leaves hills distances and time

burning the text and the hands that wrote the text

burning history and all the houses of chronology and debt

burning simply burning until everything has disappeared

though burning still through all the conceivable eons

that have come and gone in the empty vastness of the heavens

infinity is what's left over

12-27-21

EPITAPH FOUND ON A DESERTED WINTER TRAIL

infinity is the space between numbers one and two

to what avail the sun with his seven horses ?

the celestial dancers have lost their cloud-stuff

horizons are no longer discernible

east becomes west north turns into south

I will never read *that* poem again with its structures

of grass and ivy and its forlorn tenses

had we but known what was going on

the great Wheel of the empyrean revolves no more

sky is an abstract noun fulfilling no one's desires

bees turn away from the objects of sense

can words ever come to life again ?

where are the stairs that once stood here ?

the bridge to the stars the hands that guide

apostrophes and asterisks accent marks that climb

into some vast and empty parenthesis

cast aside new clothes and credit cards !

ponder the moon's next unscheduled moves

who lies here unmarked and unmourned

once ran the fields with heat of joy and leaped

as if to touch the inevitable doorway of Fate

when did he disappear in what forgotten month ?

eternity's single moment pivoted in the insect's eye

and cities both remote and undesigned toppled

in the pronunciation of the void and alas

what steps he ran what shoes and combs

what elastics and hoops to capture the waning air

all gone ! from here to the next forbidding life

the endless mile that exists between two blades of grass

unmeasured loss of the finger in the twilight lawn

wayfarer ! if you travel this far and wonder

whether the glass still reflects or the winds

have consonants that bind – consider the unseen gods

their wains and vessels and ruptured icons

all turned to dust like red powders scattered

in the archaic moment when time stood still

on its phonetic pinnacle of grief and longing :

planets lost their way sun never more rose from his bed

can words ever come to life again ?

12-28-21

THE ANTICLIMACTIC YEAR 2021

the superb angels of death tawny as lions

and with bloodshot eyes appeared before noon

drawing with them wintery breath and darkness

house after house quaked with invisible fear

and open-space markets with awnings capsized

and the people a-fright running all directions
such the epic start to time's endless final day
niches of infinity and arroyos where galaxies
drown their specious lamps sputtering ashes
as sulfur rains and lightning bolts forty years
in length turn the clouds into fiery hailstones
and earth multiplies itself in false mirrors
planet supreme among lesser asterisks and
boudoirs become a riot of gala shows glittering
with advertised promises of tinfoil paradises and
salvation a hundred brooding inches above
Gaia's turbulent and erupting volcanic skin--
sent by Pluto death's enormous seraphim shake
with ire their pleated black wings that reduce
shining metropolises to dung hills and cinders
and what of the innocence we shared in oblivion's
sweet playground when years were but grains of sand
and for this I cry out the names of *my Dead* the
inarticulate and the early damned in the process
of breath's give and take those for whom x-ray
and sad prognosis was the seal and revelation
and memory in its slotted inches of insanity but
a movie reel caught flapping uselessly on the spool
can I name them ? do the syllables that echo
resonating in the galactic mire mean anything ?
the world's controversies and hedonism are
dominion and the continents shifting on their

thin shelves send infrared messages to the moon !

like the day in General Hospital under sheets

of gravity and illusion when the *Beloved* expired

clutching to her breast a visible copy of Spain

the rest is indiscriminate rock fragments put

on trial fossil and leaf-bed and isolation ward

the immense and futile conjecture of infinity

in what region of the heavens are we traveling ?

how can we obtain eternity and still be alive ?

what divine playwright has set these wheels in motion

such that no dust arises and even air remains untouched ?

facing the sun's darkening homophone with pure

immobility *mind* simply dissolves

absence is the essence and be-all of desire

as the year comes crashing to its projected end

a conclusion and corruption of unfinished letters

silencio !

12-29-21

A LESSON IN CLOUD PHYSICS

interstices where dissolved vowels are redesigned

pure sound the trek through the heavens on

the chariot of infinite rebirths and ambidextrous

sun wheeling his seven black steeds around

the indefinite spatial curve enjoins us mortals to hold
steadfast to our allotted deaths and great spirals
of light pyrotechnics of the upper spheres and Lo
do we hear the voice of Plato in their midst a diagram
of grammatical pauses and the syntax of ideas circling
so much and so little to consider in the famous instant
when eternity doubles itself flashy igneous instamatic
as a photo of absolute light the soul itself phosphorescent
and et cetera the philosophers on their stone blind
to the portents in the sky and cloud weft and woof and
sleep in the grain our troubled brains struggling with
waking and nonsense the trace that leads east to the Mountain
where Buddhas up to a thousandfold tend to *silence*
becoming in a succession of eons amphibian and tree
and bridge-builder and tonic accent the literature
of noise and absence abrasive and puny histories
eventually the chronologies of thought wayward
in a magnetic field that destroys whatever comes into
its orbit and ask ourselves how can we ever understand ?
take my hand Cupid ! it's all in the Sanskrit dictionary
as complete a repertoire of the Possible yet devised
we are left clinging to adolescence and the little rules
that govern grass between seasons and lipstick and drugs
that alter what the eye imagines is in front of it !
imagine ! and the directives from the source of Light
and the dreams interwoven between retroflex consonants
and the subtle matter that seems to exist between numerals

and then where are we walking backwards through a glass
refracting waters both visible and invisible and charity
to recognize among each other the one who is and
the one who will never be
12-29-21

THE NIGHT JOE DIDN'T COME HOME, or
THE ORIGINS OF HARMONIC CONVERGENCE

still waiting and Joe still hasn't come home
all night no I don't know why or when he is
except I think he went to that jazz joint
on 63rd street below the elevated like the last
time when he showed up before dawn without
his shoes but this time it's different and the hours
don't end and night is an eternal blur a spectrum
of stars mostly dead rank with glowing plutonium
from five billion light years off and the whiz
whirr and buzz sound in the head tells me
some kind of telepathy you know he was always
somewhere in fourth dimension space travel
with ideas about where time leaves off and something
quite different takes over a big noise and revolution
of circles and wheels and suns full of amphetamines
all that karma and reincarnation stuff rankling within
it was the peyote I think started it and the LSD in Paris

when he woke up in a hospital bed and didn't know
how he got there or falling down a hill in Greece
breaking an arm and drinking ouzo beatnik dharma
bum that he was in those days of course and but
lyric poetry to the contrary and the high Himalayan
alert to the senses equaled only by how much alcohol
he could contain and woman after woman but never
could get back to that primal innocence he yearned
back in the twelfth grade and I can't get over
the feeling that this time something much worse
has happened to him not just falling off that little
wooden wagon in Culver City when he chipped
a bone out of his noggin and Sis had to carefully
reinsert it do you suppose something happened
to his thinking then a good question or when he
steered his sled into the trunk of an apple tree on
Saint Mary's hill one afternoon and I had to drag
him half unconscious back to Granny's all sorts of little
incidents like that smoking pot on rooftops before
sunrise listening to Sun Ra or Miles and being greater
than he was or could ever be trying to slash his wrists
on broken glass and causing such a ruckus on campus
dodging the fuzz and sitting there giggling Sunday
afternoons in a red wine and marijuana stupor
Jesus Joe come off it where the hell are you now ?

12-29-21

TIME'S FALSE DEMARCATIONS : NEW YEARS EVE 2021

not whole beings but relics of medieval dialects
half-visible shapes kept alive by memory and
all that circles mindlessly in the atmospheres
would that a form of stasis and permanence
prevailed and that moments of eternal longing
with their heart-felt shortened summers were
forever and a day and not just the phonetic
dissolution of entities that haunt dreams with
reverse photographic techniques and grief and
sorrow distances that exist between two letters
of an unwritten alphabet the seemingly remote hills
where leaves talk to missing gods and lawns fold
in the absence of hands to keep them and so much
else in the realm of myth magic and bedlam fantasy
mirrors and windows obscured with dark matter
the single instant of realization when sky and sea
coalesce to destroy each other on an indistinct horizon
I weep ! only yesterday mother's disembodied shift
dallied a moment beside me and her fingers tapped
the table's Spanish Braille with evangelical typography
she simply disappeared leaving no message no sign
that this had ever happened a warning to all that
mind is an error of thought a brooding remnant
in bas-relief of cities built of sand and shadow

the lengthening diphthong of histories long forgotten
of tree and slope and elevated swings that fly
toward some undesignated quarter of the heavens
where past events play with telephones and ears
to make redundant sound recordings of time
whose vain assonance goes lost in frozen galaxies
so it is today when metaphysics and philology have
no effect on the great lexicons that pass into silence
and whatever mother whispered in her departure
will never be fathomed except as a punctuation
between lives and universes of breath and light
small tattoo and lamp-wick growing dim among
years that never were and years that can never be

12-31-21

NEW YEARS DAY 2022 :
AUTOBIOGRAPHIOCAL FOOTNOTE

i

someone asked me what it was like to be a twin
lots of inexact punctuation and stammering between
the interstices that separate breath from light :
Joe came out of the womb 10 minutes before I did
 we were *identical* twins, which gave the grade
school teachers the heebie jeebies ...

and if asked who was the mad twin

we answered in the same voice *I am*

we loved each other and as kids we were Inseparable

we got scholarships to 2 different colleges as freshmen

but we couldn't take the separation and

the following year both entered the Univ of Chicago

and initially slept in the same bed

and listened to amazing south-side blues artists

shouting it out on those little 45's

then I was the first to marry

a Holocaust survivor named Claire Birnbaum

both of us too young

and too dumb to know better

and I think the separation began there

the real split took years to accomplish

gradually Joe's madness began to look more formal

with a PhD in Art History and a set

of wild theories about art and the universe

I became a librarian ...

despite the distance whenever we met up again

which became more and more rare

we became the adolescent bad boys

we always were ...

we always were

ii

But today Joe it's both different and the same

we are sitting at a table facing each other

waiting for the clock to hit midnight
a bottle of booze between us which we methodically
consume one glass after another gazing
into the strange universe in one another's eyes
will it be Scheherazade or Bolero the last notes
we hear before blanking out and winding up
at the Valencia dance hall bouncing up and down
with red-heads in silver spangle form-fit dresses
and everyone going crazy kissing and slobbering
into the early dawn of time when Neanderthal
projections of linguistic excess and the charivari
of the illuminati guide us into some equally distant
dusky and timeless cosmos when the future
actually precedes the past and clairvoyant with some kind
of Mayan space-travel design carrying us in and out of
whatever knowledge we were meant to comprehend
wasted as we were and continue to be and hands
that ache to remember and hair-line pomaded
and pink shirts and ivy-league ties supposed
to fool gate-keepers that we were older and
beyond adolescence and the shoe-polish and spit and
fermentation of thoughts in our puerile map-obsessed
brains and the reveries of idealized cities built
on the shorelines of space and the oceans
running up to grab our knees and someone
dumping us unconscious into the back seat of a sedan
yeah Man that was cool all right and the good
Lutheran reverend who advised our mother

what did he know of what was going to happen next

that was New Years 1955 perhaps

and today four thousand and a million more

light years later fumbling galactic interchanges

trying to somehow reach you and hug your very

visceral presence if it's still there voice and

shadow waving an outline of early philosophy which you

read to an audience of girls wild to have just a part

and so it is you are here as a hologram

your eyes locked in mine as we methodically

divide that bottle of booze between us

waiting for the next midnight

the one that never comes

iii

French illusionism painterly heat-strokes yellow

beyond all imagination fields with human-voiced crickets

maze of grass and leaf intaglios of sky captured

in its inch of eternal noon and hiking out to riverbanks

infinitely longing for what can never be and reciting

unwritten poems in ancient dialect of stone and hedge

colored rocks and gravel and wheels forever immobile

what it was like to be a twin

01-01-22

THE INEFFABLE & ETERNAL MOMENT

the very bitter and indescribable more like longing
than shadows of words ineluctable presences
in the splintered memory of passing through this
was once a life a lived presence waking and walking
beside trees and their ineffable souls to commune with
only air and its azure ghost and listening as a secret
water rushing underfoot and the free-song of distance
the terrible inability to explain and understand what
the every remoteness was that tilled the mind's back
thoughts the hovering cloud-warp before the eye
like music which has nothing to describe but a cosmic
nuance shivering where did it go was I here before ?
nothing to set down on paper no syntax to ascribe
a spectral nonchalance of sounds coming from the hive
where summers hibernate generating phantoms
copies of disembodied children doing the roundelay
of time back and forth between the pages of a book
no one has ever read let alone written the fantasy
and monopoly of the heavens chance stars and asterisks
fortunes of rock and gravel the extensions hands
yearn for in the redundant evening of the ancestors
a telling without a tale motion and gravity of sleep and
the dissension of a horizon glimpsed just once with
its mountain and steeple and the ding-dong of late
afternoons looking for a way home
01-01-22

WHAT THE SPHINX SAID

do you not speculate on the source of color

the spectra that band across the eastern Mountain

and the days as they come and go are they not

the only day and how to count past three

and to train the mind to emptiness letting

wordless thoughts pass into sleep and waking again

is that a sort of rebirth and how to account for memory

the sport of nymphs and water lilies the ponds

that dot the story-teller's hillsides and the art

of putting shape to stone and adoring the likeness

of deities placed on walls or simply in meditation

do we then still puzzle at the sky's eternal redundancy

is memory not at play in all we see and beckon

from the alerted winds and the empire of leaves

that surround almost all we cultivate and to erect

structures with entrances but without exits and

suddenly to wonder that we have crafted speech

out of the noise and nuisance of sound and call

that poetry the evocation of memory and sorrow

that attends the life of man the passage through

anterior lives if that be so and consider also this

that in the end when hues and distances have been

numbered and a scale has been set to approach

the heavens and to ponder whether in those vast

regions lie the origins but a whim it is all this science

this failure to organize the least error and hearken

back to childhoods and the darkness deep within

loneliness at the root and the meandering lamps

and signals that coruscate along the way to what

avail the conclusion to light and the ambiguities

what is greater than the rumor of transcendence

the longing and bereavement that distinguish man's

lot and refuge and subordination to higher goals

principles of of misunderstanding and subterfuge and

always the eye searching scouring the spatial altitudes

between breadth and width and the immediate sense

of dying before it is ever really comprehended

01-02-22

THE BLIND-SPOT

for Ali Memarsadeghi

suspended between a verbal clause and the opening
of space mind reiterates retracts and stammers
tottering over thought-ruins relics of an unremembered
past the gateway to oblivions new and old the sections
once meant to be read now effaced and left to molder
in an unused past tense even as youthful sounds emerge

copies of an event horizon a distance dreamed but not
realized as we the others of an abused pronominal system
consider ways to apportion the constant eternal present
among the conjoiners of infinity a rectitude that borders
on living philosophy the numinous and numerous infinities
projected by our casual and often wayward reminiscences
or is it simply that we are effigies proceeding through
mirrors spectral absences of fictitious personae residue
of mask and glove the opportunity to at last abandon
language for something like the silence of gravity as
planets plunge from sight and the license to identify
dissolves into integers both cyclopean and invisible
the very numbers that can no longer create their own
aura indivisible phantoms of birth longing and regret
fountains of reverie and inaction the extended afternoon
of a summer in the antipodes of childhood both rumor
and error infinitesimal noises of the insect world mining
the lush cornfields of July before revolving back
into the primordial darkness from which such notions
are spun and Lo ! the crevice that separates the *now*
from the *actual* widens splits further and divides
the entire cosmos into irrelevant hemispheres
and then you or I it is immaterial which pilots for
a very brief instant the balance between logos and death
we measure nothing so much as the delicate surface
where our beings intuit a physical difference or

the collision between unexpected universes and it all

comes back to this moment the two of us conversing

at a café across from the Anthropology Department

in a system of horizons and interactions of the Unknown

a supreme and gorgeous blind-spot of recognition !

01-02-22

A HOMERIC THRENODY

bristling spears and flanks of shields midst

what tongues can do displaying dark clouds

of thought the minions in the woof of battle

fear-spun and delving deep into the paginated

fray from afar espy paired vultures perched

on the royal oak mission from Zeus the silver-

bowed archer solar deity Apollo in such guise

just out of school the bell an echo in the spent

ears listening intently for the sky's cracked

vase or an overture in the delphic style hailed

their diminutives aloft hand and metal coursing

like mists and what a noise the shouts and glee

girls tossed into the crowds shift and blot hasten

to cover the sun's imminently blackening vowel

louder than before and the suddenly human

wall Greeks no less in their Ionian dialect cries

to besiege before sundown the battlements of

the lofty citadel line after line of hexameter and

the bellows fast at work in the smithy forging

weaponry and armor not to mention coining

new words sounds beyond buzz and whirr thick

with consonants dredged from Egypt and waste

of night-spell stars luminous for a moment only

betokening the souls departed of the bereaved

warriors in their grammar-book lesions spelled

in an archaic series of symbols and notches

painted bright red on the new pottery their

illumined faces descending to Hades and bright

but barely legible names theirs in a script

borrowed from boats-men from eastern shores

a mountain of text unsigned the rolling waves

wine-dark the spilled brains egress and totem

in scansion fingering syllables like summer grass

then evening comes the soil rich with blood and

entrails to be read for the future and eerie songs

nocturnal birds with fierce yellow eyes and series

of destroyed bodies piled one upon the other did

I know any of them ? life's bitter toll among them

the absent and missing strangers of childhood

sent to the front with headlines of glory the savage

inconsolable language that is dread and strife

to be mourned as strophes in a foreign idiom

wafting sprites in hills dotted with leaf and silence

for whom the lamp shone ever too briefly

for whom there was no promised other day

01-03-22

GRIEVING THE HUMAN CONDITION

everything ends and each day is death-defying

nothing more to be written nor spoken out of turn

no school to attend no library's knowledge to sack

a gathering of deaths light rain forecast talking

still through the endless night a sequence flashing

of images archaic and poignant did we ever really ?

situations of light faltering between doubts of --

in pursuit of a renewed definition of language

puzzle and enigma miscommunication and slander

tragedy is at the root of grammar as sky's multiple

twin looms even darker if to wake is a subordination

of rules and to move through error the foundation

to observe the faulty stars casting fates the number

it takes to disbelieve and the boomerang and hand

it casts and shadows removed from mirrors daily

the redundancies of sound captured in wax and myth

who is retelling the same old tale as age sets in

the reiterated compassion the advice and source

of recriminations like headlines mistakenly printed

about annunciation and debt neon graphics displayed

in a theater where everything goes into stasis a warrant

for arrest a pugilistic encounter with a back-alley god

confusion and aphasia startled to be alive after

such an illumination counting backwards in trance

the moment of articulation before consciousness took

over the settling and consummation of identities

noise in the left ear the echo of ancient seas roiling

bark and chaff detritus and immolation fumes

rising in the toll of uncounted days the newly dead

in their southland of reproach and inconstancy what

is an event what does it matter in and out the same

door revolving portal of misgivings and memory

perpetuation of fragmentary thinking asleep at

the so-called wheel divorce and realignment of brides

altars fused to the number four and air knotted

into epicycles and someone behind the screen going on

about what is to occur if something doesn't give

such is the quotidian cosmos the meridian of statues

monopoly of stone and atmosphere is it a wonder that --

childhood consumed in the profligate instant of loss

then does grass hush and grieving forget to speak

01-04-22

FELIZ AÑO NUEVO !

rainbows of breath ! the isolation ward fills with rust
and choleric mortals plead another minute no less an hour
of aggravation and futility and mythologies fade across
the frosted windowpanes a lesion in geography a map
of dissension in diphthong and circumflex the language
attributes of a halcyon archaic period dissolve in a spectrum
held up to the light shadowy hands and flinging aside
bodies of evidence the witless and despondent x-ray that
reveals just how much history has failed inspiration and
then fellow travelers in their incubators align thoughts
with small promises to revive by noon when statuary and
solemnities of sound correspond to planetary ellipses
how immense and distant is the mountain's syllabary
the treacherous ascent to a form of belief that transcends
and so many bodhisattvas caught in a highway pile-up
outside the nation's capital and streaks of ruddy lapse
sky gathers its knots and clouds the eyes with redundant
lightning and theatrical booms that shudder the nerves
an afternoon suspended in the twisted branches of time
which experts in drugs and ink-blot tests survey the damage
to so many humans inhibited by fear of dying and immolation
the pyres mount up in the suburbs where one-eyed prophets
explicate random series of disease and legend the Athenian
constitution the Zoroastrian eternal flame the box hidden
in Grand Central Station episode of Pandora and the demons
all out affront to reason and dignity the charade of politics

the assembled books that cannot be translated to heaven
blinded angels and cherubim wings blackened by the sun's
deadly homophone litter the transepts of the upper air
with fossil debris of thought inklings of immortality
multiplied copies of a single mirror in which everything
possible has happened and the revolution of glass and
antinomy generating enigmas and pyramids music from
a thousand and eight years ago and assassinations unrecorded
by the knife and idiom of literature et cetera the world
today as never before on its own edge about to plunge
like ink into the deluge of even blacker cosmic waters
a finger ! a blade of grass ! integers of vowels inserted
between the amnesia and aphasia of leaves longing as ever
for the silence that passes understanding

01-05-22

HYMN TO THE *PARCAE*

from the solemn century of grief past
parenthesis and failed destiny the sword
naked in its steel of intent the basilisk to kill
offend the dark and undo the cosmic sutures
designed by *the sisters three* revolving their
wheel the loom with invisible fingers to ply
such ancient misconstrued eventualities now

come to be the deaths more than multiple
on roadsides strewn and sun's oblique patent
dim recollection of light the dun and grey
hills that mark the faint dialects of man aside
the whispered sorrows the stones that mark
some archaic moment is it anything but an
accident the error of pride and masquerade
the ego's pointless posturing heroic or absurd
come patient and silent to this other side
be under this tree's shady borrowing a soul
to remember all things come to this point
and not grasped simply disappear in the vale
that lies below our feet the dark domain
of Persephone and her ill-bruited mate
god-of-underneath the demon of ideology
do summers retrieve their golden flights
their swarms of illusive memory or is everything
the wreckage of a marble block fallen
from the heavens that exist far beyond
the map's most remote limit the mountain
of pure solitude and mourning the abacus
and calculation of the aimless stars
once thought to be the abode of those
lost along the way their frail resonance asleep
like asterisks on the fading screen of time

01-06-22

ODE TO JANUARY

of matters the most a street in time

the cuneiform of clouds the deconstructed sky

a length to pass before another room begins

and dark the obsolete and fuming distances

night swallows in a wink the burdened semaphore

misdirected traffic of all-souls however much

the past reconvenes on its solitary peninsula

a shape of air a division of the atmosphere

into halves that do not match and so much more

the brain cannot conceive the sleeping galaxies

in their mired evolution of gas and inconsistency

and mists and moats and jugglery of light-beams

aimed at the sun's internal blackened homophone

vowels that turn into hyacinth and narcissus

and statues born from consonants that open

the gates of inferno to the misguided and what dolorous

chasm of tribulation this human moment turns out to be

a face turned to glass some emotions gone awry

and multiples of the single half one accepted as

the gift of breath and anon to hills in the smuggled west

with vespers and alliances with the darkened host

this month cursed with its nocturnal infinities

star-spent welkin tremulous and ethereal as

the alabaster adornments of a fictitious queen

however many the reductions of space to its inch

and the halcyon islands adrift with their Homeric poem

and childhood rueful reminder of death and dying

as it approaches the abyss in its feminine form

this welter of useless days and mourning forever

the irreparable losses of life and memory

to what end the penultimate syllable exposed

to the faint assonance of a solo instrument playing

in the infirmary of missing hands an anonymity

finally of mask and pronoun the identity of no one

lying abed beneath an infrared exposure to the beyond

January ! monstrous introduction to still another cycle

of days copied from now defunct galactic routines

semblances of self in a broken mirror suspended

somewhere between the thumb-nail and its excursus

depths intaglios residual fault-lines insanity

the tiny bedlam of insects looking for a granary

the mind ! labyrinth of concupiscence and void

hours that slip like alphabets of absinth through

hendecasyllables of classical detritus and shipwreck

month of too many months ! January of longing

birthright and totem beast with whom I sleep

the frozen dot dot dot of a geminated code

mon fils

01-07-22

UPON HEARING OF EVEN MORE DEATHS AND THE YEAR HAS SCARCELY BEGUN

to translate the mystical sound one needs

not ears but a heart full of sand a shuttle

that moves mysteriously from right to left

to deny the sun's origins in adamant rock

and to quarry from pre-dawn air the shape

of the secret letter written so no one can read it

it is to mourn Adonis by the dry well with women

whose faces are the very symbols of enigma

knowing that among them Aphrodite shifts

from tawdry burlap into untinted threads

torn from a loom of ink and to listen intently

to her warbling muffled sobbing like a sea-bird

lost in the mists of time and to realize this noise

is the very antiquity of sound the depths and abyss

of the human condition inscribed in clouds that

neither move nor remain still yet lose and regain

their formations in the ear of the mountain erected

on the eastern rim of earth's archaic bowels

today is no better no different from that moment

transcendental and unique and unrepeatable

despite the sonorous redundancies of a sea wave

interred in the mind's small pink shell as if to

create a new orient of music inaudible and high

dilating between the various Syrian skies of Genesis
and the sacrificial altars that lie in ruins outside
imaginary cities of clay and wattle and through
which a traffic of metals and digits and buttons
with no known use rattle and flicker malfunction
and entropy the untouchable engine of death
moon-spans and pyramids longing for renewed
distances of shale and lipstick the cursive wrap
of mummies made to sit and observe their pasts
before the future of memory displays itself like
a Tibetan banner of yellow silk that takes the wind
and reinvents it with lost dreams and dialects
everything unravels in the hands that waking
struggle to remember the porous cloisters of sleep
inch and diameter of space-before-time and hues
radiating from a shapeless wheel dazzle and it
is here in the inconstancy of movement that
the immense and invisible sorrowing takes place
today at noon in front of the decaying courthouse
the summons to gather the meridian planets
and their failed daughters the woebegone lakes
the statues of pure incompletion the myths and
dislodged vowels the hair-pieces of empire and
finally the numbness of the bride in her album
was anyone ever more unconscious and between
this instant and the loss of recognition and the

futile efforts to revive anyone it all comes to

end in a half-recalled voice on a phone saying

something incomprehensible and the fading

phonetic structures dissolving in the grasses

where are laid to rest the missing fingers

integers of the annual deaths of Adonis

AOI

01-08-22

EPILOGUE—JOE GOES DOWN UNDER

the rest follows no film can make

a breath intake some scattered lights

for a blank an instant and weeds overgrown

musk and distant fragrances soil overturned

the worm and his metallic gaze the world burns

to no one and for no reason sky gathers

its ruffled silks and transpires a lessened

tense the various pasts and describe what

no sleep applies the diverse figures of a play

performed but once and since forgotten

you and I slight arabesques in a fogged mirror

first to go through the unknown gate you

turned and smiled the winds that grabbed

you by the hair the extent of an hour suddenly

dismissed and statues placed on the right

where the park is stifled with weeds and dandelions

you stomped your foot and down came the curtains

what a voice flickered in the ear a hoarse maze

of consonants and interrupted vowels

a decade of insane years but a matter of minutes

and now your bride is gone as well into that

infernal cloaca of gassed stars and asterisks

mispronounced galaxies speeding their way

out of a grammar book into a luxurious extinction

what are the alarms going off this afternoon ?

a library with its decibels of unprinted matter

lexicons and word-lists and tiny illustrations

of gravity impending and the no-exit signs

in bright red where the mountain stops

loud ! infamy and jealousy and the poetry of fire

and divinity--there will never be enough !

you and I parted the moment concrete turned to ice

July and its thousand crumbling epithets

recycled heat and a corner that can never turn

multiple copies of that instant circulating

on the immense wheel of the cosmos

an afternoon composed of marble and honey

farewell --

02-09-22

ON A WINTER DAY BY PADMA-LING MANDALA
for Antonia Gustaitis

others have died before and shared in their passing

this panoramic view of San Francisco Bay and

sensed the multiplicity of phantoms winged or not

flitting in their insect differences above the man-made

illusion of skyscrapers and bridges and listened intently

to the ear of the cloud as it vacuumed the iridescent

space where sorrow both spreads and dissolves and

grief which is uppermost loses its voice and winnows

from the curved air a supreme vowel a digit of noise

like the *scree-scraw* of crows on nearby telephone posts

it is down below earth's fragile surface that the *boom*

registers its most potent tears its suffering and loss

the round table of spirits trading identities and hands

the sheer fiction of the after-life the beyond the circuit

where planets regenerate their diffused energies yet die

despite all the physics and mantras and embolisms and

fate the tiny print below the fingernails turning brown

with fear and longing in the wan hospital afternoons

when windows turn black and cry for the sun's rays

one more time and the hospice keepers look on with

prayerful eyes and murmur syllables of transcendence

and peace all in a dialect of untranslatable verbatim

the great Sanskrit lexicons jettisoned for a few meters

of soundless poetry imagery of winter branches making

appeal with their gnarled fingers to a heaven no greater

than an eyelid hovering above the gold-sculpted beasts

that dominate the silent portal of entry and departure

forever and the heart at this point opens up to a light

from afar a feeble diminishing of something glimpsed

just once in a triad of decades when laughter was a street

and everyone thought yes today is the eternity of youth

01-10-22

THE DEATH OF ELENA GUSTAITIS

I should have seen it coming the way you sat

poised on a bar stool downing a hard-boiled egg

with a long draft of beer at Jimmy's Woodlawn Tap

what must be six decades ago and even in the tarnished

glare your skin with its borrowed amber dredged

from the Baltic Sea shone and your laughter

infectious peals from the caverns of some divinity

it crystallized there the alcoholic physics lessons

the empyrean of French art history with its

monologues of irreverent suns and marigold distances

and you fell for all of it in the guise of my brother

that truant of intellect and mysticism tirading

against the bourgeois and the American flag and
the conventions of German philosophy mirrored
in the smoky haze of an endless drinking bout that
moved from room to room and into the street
and finally into your bed on the Westside of Chicago
where lawns bristled with notions of private property
and fears of World War III echoed in East European accents
the Luftwaffe must have been hovering ghostly
above the deadly nightshade you and José trampled
in frenzied ecstasy devoted to an academic Dionysus
and just so you endured the trampolines and
penny-whistles the cart wheels and the beach skits
only to wind up dumped in a Lake Michigan maelstrom
the lesson was to eke out your own career in fierce
bronze sketches of years to come in Navajo dust and
unrelenting midwifery an unabashed Buddhist
inclination to sound out the minds of others in pleats
of disregard for propriety and a total dedication to Beauty
when news of your death reached me unexpectedly
by phone I was immediately reminded of news of José's
imminent death by phone and the two of you
then and there were remarried in a nocturnal confusion
I cannot shake your laughter your irreverence your ambergris
delicacy of thought coiling around asterisks of space
the barroom physics lessons cigarette after cigarette
that was what killed you and the choreography

of your youth the ballet of cuneiform and hyacinth

the histories of virtually all the doomed nation-states

the remotest and most proximate of planets that tilted

warily but gracefully in your dreaming eyes

and the cinema of so many disconnected moments

like the time in south Berkeley when you recorded

my poem for a short film called

Amérique mon coeur perdu

01-10-22

THE POISONED TREE OF WORLDLY EXISTENCE

"...la prison terrestre où nous sommes jetés"

Charles Cros

you look in the mirror and examine a rose

lawns engender frost and skies crumple in a fist

distances between thirst and desire doubt and envy

wither with reports of a thousand years of dying

not once did the raised finger avail nor the grasses

that cling to lordly domains of worm and midge

do anything to stay the dark spread of oblivion

cling to one fruit savor its inexplicable poetry

or choose the other shining plum to understand

there is no company of good men nor prosperity

in the gilded coin only ransacked histories

lakes of mirage and rattled silences like winds

that devour mountains in a trice or the words

of promise and troth between lovers behind

their masks and what else is there but harvest

of deaths in the headlines or on radios beamed at

Mars while sulking in her mesh of bright aluminum

Venus gnaws her knuckles weeping bitterly the buds

of flowering youth mowed down by the machine gun

of ideas and misdirected thought and of the forest

attended by the mind's savage beasts leafy bowers

the reign of absence and isolation do we there trust

to go and seal our souls with penance and misery ?

to be born and breathe to rave wildly at the light

to fling spears with hopes of downing the sun's

immortal homophone and write in hieroglyphs

of perfume and drugs raw experiences of youth

and yet come to terms with nothing the blank

wall that mortals besiege for dumb glories

the thumb and ear the ventricle and harmonium

choices to be loud with soundless pronouns or

from the fray retreat and lose the hands in a game

of chance the roulette of despair and chicanery

what is the lesson of the nocturnal telephone

the unbridled grief the information of still another

death added to the uncompounded number that

cannot be calculated the heights of space in an inch

the fix of gravity and the solemnities of sleep's

immaterial depths eternities of the single moment

when time and memory coalesce explode and

dissolve in the multiple infinities of the leaf

01-11-22

DON'T ASK

the least word like snow dissolves in the wind

of the centuries awaited by so many spent candles

the day a minimum of light the charity of blind gods

the ages have passed over the immobile eons of stone

grasses work their way into what the eye used to see

the head of its own accord listens but hears nothing

of the dying crickets or wounded flies the air is a-buzz

with hives of distance smoke and wine and refugees

pleading for a passage though the mountain whose

hands have long since ceased to exist and borderlines

erased by a single stroke of gas the essences of space

have long been extinguished gutters and curb-sides

where linger phantoms five-fingers each and crying

within the glass hidden behind the lost summer's

eternalization a fox and flame a tinder-box a noise

at the very end of sleep inaudible as sorrow underneath

the quilted patch that disguises the reticent dawn

to wake again ! a cheat a threnody a puzzling line

of poetry brought to bear on the sun's loud escapade

years are minutes in the small mirror of memory held

beside a speeding vehicle to capture something of

the blur which is the basis of cognition and entropy

the stars ! the magnets and punctuations of night

the spindrift of secret oceans racing on their knees

to reach the still-point that divides time from oblivion

a loss ! another day with its futile weeks of ennui

expectation of continents on the verge of transience

which is the language of the letter-box and perfume

the unassembled sequence of sounds that litter

the ear of sand adrift on its own peninsula of water ?

the hills where the clock's dialects are buried and

the lesser path that leads straight to the infernal portal

with its redundant footsteps and roadside epitaphs

the scrawl of archaic pictograms about salvation

and the scrutiny of consciousness before nightfall

hush of vegetation ancient as quartz and leaves

folded in on their own unabiding silence

01-12-22

TODAY THIS ACHING

I feel a proximity to death in the very sun
whose brilliant silence is deaf as stone
in the people I meet whose faces are missing
in the way the corner turns before the car does
in the concrete lining to the sky and its distances
proximity to death in the voices that pierce the ear
with its own remote control device that
repeats and multiplies the deaths approaching
nearer and nearer to this day of all the strangest
in a symposium of triads and epithalamia
who is it whispering at me as I steer the wain
straight into the place vacated by planet Pluto ?
I am snared by a perfume called opium to a hotel room
darkened with alcohol and menstrual blood
in the month of the shattered childhood cranium
the calendar is a body of water and the years coral reefs
becoming blanched by the improprieties of time
there is a pier that aches to reach the spheres
whose noisy rout of asterisks burn like paper torches
in nights that haunt every minute of this day
with its visceral immemorial deaths that draw me ever
nearer to my own puzzle in a color of rain and sorrow
how can this grieving ever cease ?
where are the semaphores of stop and go that
signal there is no day after this ?
where is the signpost in crumbling cuneiform

that says the dream is a fringe of madness ?

there is a pier that aches to reach the spheres

and from where I stand on the hills of invisibility

the grammar of tomb and urn looms large on the rim

where the western seas inter their memories

in mountains of pre-fabricated immortality

and yet there is a smoking wheel and diverse chants

from cloudy banks and sepulchers of space

symbols of a polarity of no known place the somber

residues of redundant echo and grassy knoll

to lay the head *there* today will be no more !

01-13-22

THE POETRY WORKSHOP

"el deber del Poeta es convertir el Paraíso en Infierno"

      Roberto Bolaño, Sepulcros de Vaqueros

and we go on talking about this and that

clair de lune and the shores of love

the drunken boat and the trance-dance

we do as effigies of mirror-selves pronouns

too weak to stabilize communion with the gods

mask and foil color and fade the damnation

and salvation between one breath and the other

who I am and who you are both the wistful backward

glance into the glass only to find it empty

the residue of noise the ear impounds in the sleep

of chaos the bump and grind of sylvan nymphs

pictures of a gone world passed from hand to hand

the latest tome gift and gab of a small pocket of verse

lies and chicanery dumpsters full of hexameter

double vision of the blinded seer and yes

can clouds actually speak revealing their lack of identity ?

talking as if we understood and meant every syllable

from antiquity on and the byzantine choice

whether to genuflect or prostrate before the goddess

exchanging glove and tone making sure nothing

is in place and lifting with a single shoulder the heavens

of a cinema without origins and doubt and envy

ever with us as we pull the levers or press the button

up in smoke it all goes the old body with its poetry

of naïve despair and egregious self-pity the *arcana*

stuffed into an unaddressed envelope and left to puzzle

the one who finds it unawares or sleeping on a park bench

the riddle of life ! the thing so often discussed

we never agree we only quibble and quarrel

ere night finds us each on the other side of the divide

ranting a recitation of automatic writing stolen

from the library of perpetual adolescence

geminated consonants ! superficiality of hands !

the poet's obligation is to turn Paradise into Inferno

01-14-22

BEYOND THE *NOOSPHERE*

in the bottomlands where forests of ice and glare

converge with the light's last dwindling beams

sleep is left to drift from its galactic peninsula

into the ever more borderless empyrean

small spotted deer shock-still ears pricked

to the noise of a devastating distance and

even as memory empties its coffin of words

the end of all sound and direction the blanks

where stars used to advertise their extinctions

silence greater than all the spatial histories

of origination and destruction a single finger

extended into the hemispheres of contrition

and longing such as are myths of the dead

afloat in the somber pre-dawn of every day

remaining left to puzzle why the lesson was

never learned the story left incomplete and

the library doors forever shut and crying

on both outside and inside the phantoms who

inhabit the infinite inch outside echo's reach

walking in a dream where am I if not elsewhere

the rim of possible universes beyond the *noosphere*

falling through the subcutaneous surfaces

of a coma deep into endless summer mazes

then does the poem return to me of heat and

the destiny of grass of interpolated sunspots

and the dizzy infatuation of love's first sting

the others of *me* like uninflected pronouns who

disturb empires of dust and glass and veer rushing

into the curvature of space leaving *me* far behind

in a trail of phonetic error and disbelief twin

of a recollection suspended between the mind's

oscillating leaves of silence and aphasia

01-15-22

THE VOYAGE TO NOWHERE

El Dorados of clouds ! function of the color orange !

trumpets of foam and see-through azure infinities

today is finally tomorrow and tomorrow is truly Never

the junction between memory and grass comes full

circle on a small red wagon on a suburban street

and the mind fills with the plenitude of action and grief

one following the other on an endless cart-wheel

wherever it goes it cannot say unless to sleep again

the enormous void that requires no adjectives

the extension of a hand that seeks its own design

in the luxury of a Dravidian rain-forest of syllables

what echoes of ear ! what inconsolable finalities !

perpetuity of the vowel that stands for alpha in

the scale of unities that cannot be perceived but

in the whorl of destinies perpetuated in a thunder-clap

what is a summer day ? the dozen raindrops that

compose a window and the dizziness of a slope

down which kids roll topsy-turvy into eternity

first it is Greek with a hundred divisions of air

then it all descends like a puff of steam into some

undesignated quarter of night and oblivion

with its unparalleled knees and the oceans which

are the origination of everything where the body

shores up its latitudinal dimensions and the weeping

from shoulder to shoulder—remember ? holy

the indivisible thought that goes out as the last

and only remnant into the galaxies and leaf

and coil and the smaller engines of immortality

shadows ! whatever is invisible is greater than

matter and each day is a fiction of ego and sense

we are never to arrive ! the planets spinning out

of control in their impossible court-house noon

heat-stroke and tenderness the head adrift archaic

as stone where it rests for the remainder of time

01-16-22

A LOVE SONG

the dictionary definition doesn't apply

love is neither the never nor the forever

of what happens when planets from

opposite universes collide in a dream

either one is having of the other come

the light of day and finds them sparring

with grass and leaf and memory of this

day is erased no sooner does it occur

the frieze of distance and longing a

faint recollection of remote peaks and

myths of ink and alabaster and coffins

that emerge suddenly from vows and

promises of a time to come and tongues

and tokens of misspoken sounds idioms

of eye-patch and threnody the everlasting

and buried deep beside the heart's secret

is a sound from the epoch of light when

skies were doubled by nightfall and soft

and the moon evanescent and yellow re-

emerging from the left ventricle all

big and unbelievable like a song that

catches the ear and won't let go a swoon

and trance we go together embraced

in love with love the noise of fire-crackers

in a lake and silver ebbing shores dying

in the mists and a kiss a perfumed phase

a litany and mantra abiding in a place

where rocks were born and the flood

of flowers and hills removed slowly from

the apogee of existence dialects unformed

the head grown heavy with recollection

of a single leaf vibrating in the dark

01-17-22

THE HUSH OF A FORGOTTEN SUMMER AFTERNOON

is there anything in the sky that looks like the world ?

hues blend with distant sounds the echoes of summers

all but forgotten in their raiment of testimonial cloud

and sudden thunderstorms that catch us unawares

half-way between childhood and death and the sheen

of metal moving too fast down the road and shrubbery

holy and pliant marking the edge of infinity in a park

is it a wonder all recollection is a confusion of tone and

accent and the exciting blur of faces adolescent and

betrayed by the calendar becomes a footnote in sleep

we raise our arms to that irretrievable moment when

the sun's immense and blackened fuse detonated and

took the mind from itself in the struggle to comprehend
the *other*! after too many decades the diminished light
the accolade put aside in the ditch and dump of time
listless characters scrawled on a vanishing page who
they are is a matter of conjecture some still talking
others in some sort of trance fade into the pallor of
a late afternoon memory hills and trees dense with
verdure the flicker of the eye as the air's sudden
motion blinds leaving the landscape denuded of
property and gravity the immense nothingness of
a photographic negative and a choir of crickets
submerged in the fast moving summer momentum
breath and click heat and sweat the smothered sky
revolving in its eternal and insensible circularity
you were there *Mary Lou*

01-18-22

ACCOUNT OF A FLIGHT TO LOS ANGELES ca. 1988

they put us on an airplane early in the morning
festive sounds of French illusionist poetry recited
by the hostesses in brand new azure spit-suits preening
as they walked the runway toward self-exile and we
startled still asleep like ears of solid rock dumbfounded

that we were entering no less than the sky Olympian
and cloud-clotted masses albescent tufts of galactic
matter the resonance of an eternal engine buzzing both
loud and muffled the gangplank and the sealed windows
and the captain alert in his caffeine-brandy haze warning
about take-off the bright and iridescent moment before
sunrise the destructive enterprise of Light and its inhibitions
planetary suppositions about the soul and space-travel
and memories of a library down below with illustrations
of jungles pyramids and sacred seas about to split in two
an unconscious magician and the test of identity in the air
flashes of a past that didn't belong to any of us a summer
with landscapes of quartz and hill-dialects spoken as only
statues can in dialogue with shadows intermittent and
what a moment ! something like an explosion and trays
of beverages and nuts in small packages the chatter of
trained monkeys and the Mahabharata in perfect 9th
century Sanskrit without a portfolio or lexicon teachings
of the masters what was to understand other than within
was the universe and without the congress of differences
between man woman and water the head wanting to wake
and a shining icon elevated above the aisle moving back
and forth Shakyamuni irreverent his lips still sleeping
a target of fire-crackers and whatever the hand could
devise in the somnolent journey from its anatomy into
the other side of time even as we watched eyes shut

the graceful silver wings of the plane tilt out of sight

the mantra of all-merciful Avalokiteshvara redundant

on the loud-speaker and the vigil of the body began

solemn and without memory before elisions of sound

and the noise of the ancestors patriarchal and aphasic

numb with expectation we exchanged silhouettes and

tried not to let things matter the lessons of the Upanishads

and the pre-Socratics still echoing from the evening's

concourse in the Hyatt Regency and the awful zzzzzz

demarcating the division between this life and the next

were we all going to die before getting to LAX ?

01-19-22

EXCURSUS

do the numbers add up ?

what went wrong in Hades ?

temperature rising eternal summer

July is number forty-six

the month that follows still in a coma

everything outside the window is burning

whatever remains to be seen is smoke and ashes

a green button for salvation !

a harp dispels the threat of electricity

driving a motor car through the clouds

god Pluto bewildered longs for darkness

section by section the only day that exists

falls apart in the gem-cutter's hands

a monsoon wind returns the previous month

to its pedestal lordly and virulent

green is unique among the distant hills

and a dialect of retroflex consonants

shivers in Demeter's stone ear

where is the burrow where her daughter disappeared ?

September is as a far away as the beginning of time

hold his hand ! brush his matted locks !

a divinity in sleep a precious ornament

so much weeping next to the machine

whose services are only liturgical

the third number from the left is the one

in the school photo looking all shy for the light

that penetrates to the soul and dissolves it

remember the time angel fell straight

out of a nimbus and hit the car hood ?

where were we off to that day ?

01-20-22

THINGS I CANNOT GET OUT OF MY HEAD

think of how little really matters

the ant-hill in the backyard like the inkwell

easily emptied of contents or sky

which can be overlooked falling into its own abyss

the slightest change in the thermometer

or the effusion of beta particles into the void

money ! the super-challenge of innovation

and decay the inarticulate sounds

that motivate gravity to descend leaving moon

suspended by a theory of weight not to speak

of light and its absence or is it dark and its presence ?

mothers of contention ! the nebulous content of sleep

versus the ominous vestiges of nocturnal asterisks

burning like incomplete thoughts in the back-brain

consciousness ! the flutes and aggravations

of poetry given license to abandon limits

even as running to greater waters the river

yields its opposite banks to the demon of annihilation

tiny presumptions of attitude and glory !

when breath has run its course what's left ?

one hand goes lost wondering where is its other

eye and ear fossilize in a density of unwritten memories

the alliance of scope and futility ! shadows of men

yellowing in the distant reeds of the Archaic

turn to stone and become millions of years

lost in a system of eternity and circularity

a man an integer a leaf seeking its own shape

grass ! the tender and smothering labyrinth

where fingers go missing searching the inevitable

01-20-22

HITOPADESHA

lions and tigers clever jackals

and talking bulls mice beloved of gods

and cats who reign like kings only

for a day weathers and mountains and

steep edges of the world whole realms

erased by a thumb and legends of dialects

that spring from forbidden waters

to speak and think like living mortals

statues of fluff and dust jungles too dense

to penetrate caves and hills and lanterns

that go on and off not to mention gilded fish

that learn to fly and clouds that shape

destinies of man and skies redundant and

without echo that hover over the unspoken word

fashion of tape and majesty worms and cycles

of rock and tree-root the underneath of mind

and breath exuding from imagination
so much illness and palaver so little pity
grief of passion and being born and light
interspersed between the multiple sleep
of errant planets zoographers and astrologers
mendacity of ruling monarchs ideas and fornication
adults of shadows and Chinese monograms
between the crevices of transformations birds
that guide the threads of death to newer earths
plenitude of information graphics and silence
theaters that last a lifetime to show the Mahabharata
and Krishna and his sidekick playing dice
with horses and glistening chariots and war and
its masterpieces of minister and slave
how few the lists of syllables the vowels
replete with incense and perfumes and women !
extravagances of cinema and the radio
songs that float like pyramids of celluloid
and chewing gum and fever blisters that
bring mourning to a close //
written one thousand five hundred years ago
these fables pliant and full of heresy
Buddha-types with gazes of infinity
ageless ennui of consonants
to deliver the self from feeling and the pronoun
excised forever from its tongue

01-21-22

APPROACHING STILL ANOTHER BIRTHDAY
WITHOUT JOE

in the crazy Greek book of poetry unexplained
is there hidden between the lines a Buddha of alcohol ?
I can hear the highway sound in the dark bearing us away
two by two twin after twin into the great raiment of night
blustering stars that no wind can budge glistering bright
for a moment only before falling away in the dim-lit fane
where gods who have lost somatic control of their beings fade
going away into a lackluster Elysium the boulevards
once trafficked with French theories of love now a hazy
counterpart to the event of dying the long elusive entrails
of memory where we find ourselves entwined twins to the end
puzzling over the ten minute difference that separated us
when the accident of light befell us some snowy hour
before the invention of dawn or ice and the fuming advent
of calendars carved out of stone and circular deities with
voices of immense gravel announcing that one day this will
be forgotten forever and the cherished similitude of one
to the famous other—what of that ? who would straighten us out ?
the elevator stopped at the twelfth floor and the descendents
of the tribe of *Zavuya* could only gape and stare as we
mirrored the process of reorienting the mind to subtleties
of fiction and bad poetry the raving and mantic mask
we switched now and then to fool others which one
was really you and which was never me ? knowledge was

a graft on the thin photographic plate we shared before

parting the ways and always in the gloaming distance vast

and shadowy a Buddha of alcohol was watching his eyes

tired of witnessing the obstinate revolution of unnamed planets

twins and more twins cast out by the thousands into galaxies

now long dead barely stirring in the ashes of space

this Monday where will you be ?

01-22-22

MEDITATION ON THE EPHEMERAL SELF

disarmed by Jupiter Minerva enters the dream

through the back door a bad omen a dereliction

of fate a skeletal design of space overreaching

the limits of empire and dwarfed by a stellar noise

the mortal in this dream of backward configurations

the sleeper in this lint and trefoil of inconstancy is

but a confusion of root and hallucinatory drug a spot

unable to be removed from the metallic sheen

mysteriously flashing where Minerva has stepped

trying to avoid the astrologer's predictions about

tomorrow and whatever else the text implies in

its subterfuge of oracular syllables and debate

between consonant and vowel darkness ensuing

memory's triplicate application for oblivion

what is a supernova in the annals ? where is speed

and the gravitational forces of grass the longing

and submerged dialects of twilight when voices

from the far side of time recur troubling and

infantile as if there were a duplicate self emerging

from the cocoon of non-being and birth unknown

deities at work devising a lifetime of rumor and doubt

great and erroneous passage of planet X through

pre-historic miasma rock and spurious envelope of

language spurned by water and leaf recollections

no more durable than mirror images of the past

echo and silhouette of a shadow posing as a mortal

on the wavering lawn of childhood the downfall and

rust addition to years that have no substance

so today comes as no surprise an asterisk fading

on a zodiacal chart diffused urgency of breath

nonchalant long division of the epochs that supersede

time in the long and enigmatic evolution of mind

endless thought that has no beginning even as Minerva

shuts the door to light ascending the apocryphal step

into the disintegrated unities of death

01-23-22

RANGE OF MOTION : THE POET CONTEMPLATES HIS 83ʳᴅ YEAR DUMFOUNDED IN ETHEREAL SILENCE

here I sit full in the 17th century incubator of modern music

Zefiro torna ! time's desperate inch yields to Arianna's Lament

the spool goes unwinding down red brick-paved streets

to the library or mausoleum *whichever* where the world's

poetry accumulates in countless tomes and parchment

while the sun's blind homophone suffers no variation and

the mutilated gasses of the noosphere circulate aimlessly

what is the weight of an hour ? not enough to support

the gravity of words and hieroglyphs suppurating from

the unnumbered volumes festering in the multiple basement

where intellect and razor abide side by side poring over

the totally meaningless rambling inscriptions that pass

for the anthology of all verse both written and perused by me

in moment of irreversible birth-and-death Chinese ink-block

solid red the seemingly ineradicable monument of sky

chiseled out of mind's somnolent and aphasic invention

Brother, are you listening ? this is the same poem I have

been writing ever since 1955 when I thought to be laureate

of outcast adolescent wetbacks the same indignant thought

to be more than *other* the somehow derelict and effusive

bard straddling both sides of the Greek *iota* in an effort

to obtain the ultimate note in a music that has no score

Zefiro torna ! yet another twelve-month has passed and

no nearer to the climax of the syllable than before I

surrender the *me* of all disorientation putative discord

of harmony and absence register of enigmatic *anacoloutha*

the furtive and unnoticed pronoun hidden in dialects

where hills have no attributes and the snows keep falling

and lumber and diesel fuel fill the air with strange odors

the mechanics of illusion and despair looking for a single

breach in the wall of impassivity that keeps me circling

the Mayo clinic's cold x-ray machine and puzzled forever

by the bifurcation which has separated us now eleven years

in the making and the asterisks and caryatids that glow

in the night-heavens scripted before we were born and

mother! what of her ageless and invalid Braille trying

to keep us together in torment and whiplash the seas

brocaded within her eyelids could never perfect the light

that brought us to the day of reckoning ten minutes apart

and no sooner given the prize of illumination darkened

by the avid syntax of motivation and fault the grand

and perfunctory alcohol of exhilarated forgetting !

Zefiro torna !

01-24-22

THE WORLD RACING TOWARD ITS 6TH MASS EXTINCTION

cocktail chatter unlicensed critical notes
the voices of everywhere nothing to expound
decry the poet his classical due legions of effort
to write after one thousand poems annually
the sea's silent epitaph in dream symbols
Argüelles is just a hypothesis a surreal wreck
littered among his vowels of detritus and sham
why he keeps moving shadow among whispers
denial and factual unreality the movement
to synthesize all archaic inscriptions Delphic or
otherwise he is still a sham a footnote of late
twentieth century is he like Pound or Proust !
moving on to the next room with its chandeliers
about to shatter and falling wages and price gouging
reading between the syllables of descant and lever
how he manages to fake still another pantomime
the tragedies of Momus and true-love the radio
a symphony of derelict absences and harmonies
tune it up ! pomades of hexameter and chanting
softly to the sleepers' ballad a rhetorical device
intent on delivering celestial epistles but
does anybody read him at all ? the last time
he appeared in frayed collar and denim over-skin

what a mess rockabilly falsetto of TS Eliot

overdrive with diesel fuel lyrics jump-cut

all memory and no trance the distinctions between

twin and alphabet or the even more egregious

elevation to the asterisks of certain fictional masks

worn every time he changes pronouns and the boom-box

of space he turns up the volume to hide his intellect

the sure thing is thousands of species are going extinct

almost daily and him surfing at the wheel with

sounds and words that act like sounds noise

of verbiage a veritable library of castoff Latin

dialects alpine and Balkan and medieval

troubadour wearing the wrong hat !

and license to betray penning amorous ditties

to long dead galaxies as if they were paramours

a hotel ! Buddha-types checking in and out

sophists and Dravidian retroflex personae

a jungle of toil would have us believe and on the edge

with Grand-Master-Flash and electronic sorrow

grieving the untilled furrow the abandoned leaf

the grass with its secret fingers shifting hues

evening twilight dusk the ever fading lawn

childhood vespers portrayals of sadness and *the*

inarticulate event of dying at his behest a writ

or a script of off-handed verses rectangular and

evanescent as alcohol left to dry on the road

where the principle accident occurs phonetic decay

and war looming in Eastern Europe and madmen

as always at the helm and rain forests burnt to a crisp

rivers drying up no fish left to feed the waters

bees and midges and other winged insects

monarch butterflies ! things of the past *Birds !*

and he goes on about the deaths of the precious

and the many of the few and calculus and algebra

schoolboy flings with lipstick girls chasing consonants

into the dark and the fleeting totally eternal dance

with the first love of choice centuries ago

but today ! but today ! two lone crows and a single hawk

immobile on the telephone wires above Walnut Street

echoes and lauds of Saint Francis

news is that the world is entering its sixth and

possibly last mass Extinction

01-25-22

THE DARK LABYRINTH

"Dove se ne vanno le ricciute donzelle
che recano le colme anfore su le spalle"

        Eugenio Montale, Sarcofaghi

shadow of light shadow of breath shadow of night

light that devours silence making the sky invisible

how many childhoods do you have to relive

to realize there is no past ?

it's in a blade of grass a hundred years of mourning

green fires of memory ! a stone's throw from distance

you become the passage without entrance

your hands blind and numb decomposing at each turn

of the labyrinth until what remains is the little sleep

of transfiguration that occurs when the head turns to stone

aching to know ! the dead are the better part of knowledge

the wisdom to forgive the light that betrayed

the mere outline of consciousness an alphanumeric

abscess hidden in the bone of the inarticulate body

what is the next thing to burn in the mental pyre ?

books and poems that have yet to be written

souls in discourse with souls in the long descent

to the nadir that divides space from time

at the bedside yellowing age and sweat the entrails

of nonsense obdurate fickle license to embrace all forms

rushing swoon of consciousness in white spreading

an even whiter shadow into the grave and absent void

indivisibility of the diaphanous air !

flight and fume of being in tangle of sensuous words

which are nothing but intangible husks of sound

lengthened diphthongs emerging then dissolving in

the tinder-box of existence yards opaque and dense

frieze fading on half-ruined walls of antiquity *a hill !*

asleep on the lacerated parchment of adolescence

literature indistinct and puerile zigzagging

through the tiny aperture below the pyramid of the sun

this day the color of ants and colliding electrons

expressed in a dialect chosen for its phonetic decay

and ask what is a calendar ? a score of hours

asterisks and emptied houses of the zodiac

the famous misinterpretation of speech the roundelay

of statues invoking the noontime blindness

the sun stood still overhead dumb and swart

here we *were* ! do you recall the court house

and the civil war cannon and the bells tolling far ?

that irrevocable and *impossible* instant

01-26-22

TO READ POETRY

my friend the shadow who vanished

once told me that all writing is forgery

the important thing is to begin in the middle

when all sailors are stricken with amnesia

listening to the sirens ambulances of the gods

the rest is of little matter squiggles and dots

scratches on a marble surface the decay of breath

each leaf a monument of silence like disturbances

in the dirt under the front door step

a dictionary the shade advised composed

of words that have no second letter !

of what use is vision in the forest of night

the way has never been there !

only the admonition of the vowels of angels

learning to refute the cadence of time

alone and with sorrow--the definition of memory

seas that exist only because they are pronounced !

but to read poetry ! a question of x-rays and dandelions

a foot taken the wrong direction and the sound

of invisible motors whizzing on their way to bedlam

everything must first be erased and

the spaces in between must be memorized

and a Buddha-type fourteen feet in distance

will hover at the bedstead prepared to weep

enormous hours of length and tribulation

then disappear ! you are finally dead !

echoes illusions shop-windows with toy guns !

the difficulty consists in making a page

air and its suburbs and tributaries

wind and storms tempests of marine fauna

the letter F! sleep is the critical aspect

and dreams with long syllables and short

the division between sound and meter and

the beauties as many as fit in a handful of grass

lie down and stare at the sky before it goes away

colors are redundant as are the thoughts of passage

mind ! what little of it exists is useless

a tool for re-ordering the concept of yesterday

and before you know it dead or alive

you are reading the poem you wrote tomorrow

01-26-22

THE SHIELD OF ACHILLES

the furtive delay of time iron-clad silence

outside the summer belt and stress of heat

circulating memories of the park and its vast

unlimited expanse toward the west and south

walking wasn't so nor the myth of coming home

virtually nightfall distance was everything if

the plunge and the punctuation watching the moon

pursue its own invisible red course across the

empyrean pleated and mapped against the small

back wall demarcated by a plundered garage

a whetstone wheel and empty whisky bottles

wasn't that what life was the random and puzzling

symbolic evocations of somewhere else or even

somebody who wasn't there but remembers
being an episode in street-longing the sun almost
at its zenith menacing and black in its syllable
louder than the highway sound drilling a false
prelude to the remainder of existence each of us
in pursuit of ambiguities rambling past the Greek
restaurant designated the Shield-of-Achilles cosmic
stratospheric and mysterious willing to forego
the menu and listen rapt to the inventions of
language the tongue going on about shores and
battles and greaves and litanies sorrowing how
the goddess in her raiment of spoiled light on
her knees kin to the nymphs who are watery death
like the kid who was grabbed by the diesel and
spun around to look into his eyes the immense
future of salvation fixed for all eternity a tiny
pinprick of illumination the perhaps of a month
out of order the two of us by nature animal and
fearful both the event of a split zygote and Lo!
what would ever become of the theater where
we spent long Saturday afternoons in chiaroscuro
wondering where the music came from and for
whom was the next death meant

02-27-22

THE DANCE OF THE TOMBS

sunflowers and lye-baths side by side

for all eternity memory of frolic and joust

knights and mendicants a poetry of nothing

passing from vale to vale the lives of the many

the deaths of the few the guarded silences

between fixed stars and plenty of grass

the small sleep of endeavors and talk

of days to come the lamps and lanterns

the brief flares that light the eyes with love

then die as swiftly as water in its soul

how different a window from a door or

the casual way a language shifts from dialect

to indecision lingering on hidden routes

bidding farewell to the favorite of choice

how do hair-ribbons combs and shining

pins fare cast into a mirror and does a ringing

sound its ear in alarms of piety and doom

walk carefully shun the toadstool try not

to cry each time remembrance of that time

recurs and dread even less the dark whose

invisible hands now grasp your knees

for by five you too will lie still as stone

on the marble parapet of distant hill

01-27-22

ARMAGEDDON FIRST AND LAST

weight of memories overwhelming even the sands

that are counted daily by the pyramid-gazers

as many as are the inches of space in which time

folds up to die and the glassy terraced stars

asterisks and plumes of unmitigated smoke rising

from the deaths of others the tiny fluted columns

the obelisks determined in size by ants and

cherished by all the war-drums the spangled antlers

of the Beast who dominates the mind with envy

and lust the passions paramount the color orange

and the sandalwood trees that line the distances

with versions of history nowhere to be written

and lengths of water situations and burning of

stables and cornfields and eventual summers blistering

beneath the tangent of horizontal planets swinging

into view with an eye to destruction such as great

poetry is or can be and the mammoth epicenters

just meters below the meditating glass and what of

the Buddhas four hundred million and twelve

to be exact repeating their various and unique selves

and the flaming ramparts of the cosmos existing instantly

in a dream of the poet Lucretius the oblong portals

forever shut to the vowels and parameters of song

loud the silence that exists outside eternity a fuse

and a tongue the envelope where thoughts fit

and so little else the bottom-lands the silt and

ivory the tinsel of forgetting and drugs for the

right shoulder only because of gravity a discomfit

speculation of tribes who will inherit the number four

episodes of warfare so intense only a nail file

can depict the outcome in mirrors inscribed

with legends of infinite longing and heat et cetera

tiny sublimations the recollections of twins

who haunt the pyramids of the Sun and Moon

in faraway and dusty Teotihuacan afterlife

a world that will have come and gone epochs

and glaciers the remnant of infinity

echo of leaves fading dusky like whispers

buried in an ear of stone

01-28-22

THE ANCIENT PENINSULA

the twins on their bicycles

in the early morning hours

delivering newspapers to citizens

of the nether world

and just what do the papers say ?

words archaic rock symbols air fists

struggle for survival between the one

and the two that proceeds from one

that higher than zero the next sphere

contains only nebulous content of sleep

dissemination of fractions pyres oblivion

danger in the least sound friction in the ear

lessened hills distances are only loss

longing in the twilight grasses hands

separated from their own shapes

and snowfalls destiny literature at a standstill

blank paragraphs distilled winds a mountain

no greater than an anthill but still unassailable

promises of summer recycled heat lipstick

verbiage gravel fallen leaves covering the opaque

sky the size of a dime and clouds and rumble

the remote assonance of gold louder than the sun

at its zenith when blacker than ravens

the noontime hour comes to trial phosphorous

identities and language defeated by its own omicron

devil and galactic punctuation seizures when

least expected domes photograph-albums despair

memory when nothing else weighs and depths

somewhere near the alley where it never stops raining

descent with poets to the source of names

and forgetting always why

seas are as turbulent as hospitals and daycare

futures have no verbs to conjugate the past

evidence of breath vanishing

lives ! turning invisible pages in columns

littered with dead caryatids and acanthus leaves

the ancient peninsula

the ancient peninsula

torment of the unknown and proceed

looking for the atlas of grief

01-29-22

THE LOTUS-EATERS

archangels ! police ! wake up !

lying there in tubular disgrace on some

unnamed promontory not far from wartime

excess travels sunspots drainage of breath

eloquence of those who will never stir again

fleeced by the dichotomies of life and time

whence this lethargy to ignore ?

oranges lethal dosages of opioids alphabets

which spell nothing dormers of glass

shops closed to statues with speech-defects

alarms and aphasia the longing to linger

beside pharmacies of neon and asphodel

constantly circling the starting point of amnesia

horses of make believe parading on walls

like murals depicting the last day of Troy

anklets and earrings proper to epic poetry

legions of blinded insects rotten planks grasses

left to molder in the putrid blackening noontime sun

mythographers climbing stalks in ancient fields

probing the air for carcasses of pharaohs

dynasties of musicians and cannibals

underground rivers that empty the ears of noise

while planets of pure sound circle in hospices of light

granaries of archaic rock and *hands*

above all hands ! deprived of their futures

that lie in wait for all-reviving ink

what is a mind to bear in such insolent months ?

summers that last three and a half hours

buried in tide-pools with attic coral reef

remember ? what is a dozen ? who are men ?

01-29-22

THE UNWRITTEN POEM

targets in the sky ! one two three

red and black asterisks Greek euphony

tendency to annihilate the unborn

before they learn to read

scripture and hieroglyphic dots

squiggles and hyphens that betray

meaning even as sound approaches

its new zenith in a cloudburst one

July afternoon hot and humid the degree

of memory oscillating between zero and distance

I am fourth from the left waiting

for the elevator to eternity

grass is the punctuation between childhood

and the death-bed confession

peccadilloes and out-of-control automobiles

literature in the back-seat a formidable

shade of beauty fanning and wax

the perfumes of destiny and hotel rooms

where oblivion crouches behind a mirror

with lipstick signature wave-length

the priests of Thebes were there

Haitian zombies *macumba* love !

underneath each word was a portfolio

of noise pre-recorded in Pakistan

before the partition scat-singing

Vedic funeral hymns and the barges

pulling out at the last minute from

the source of echoes and asking

is everything going to be so difficult ?

numbering the rumors and errors

you lose track of the leaves still

rustling in their existence of suspended

silence and the rattle of a lawn-mower

in a Spanish dialect of half-formed vowels

who will ever begin to write this poem ?

it is evening already in the Sierras

whispered invasions of the body-snatchers

in chiaroscuro and we sit there rapt

listening to the drip-drip in the eaves

a hand shapes a solo in the dark lawn

dewfall and vertigo total melancholy

to sleep ! night and its borderless language

of evanescent spatial craters

spreads like opium through the mind's

infinite pronouns

01-30-22

THE WRECK ON THE HIGHWAY

Who did you say it was brother?
Who was it who fell by the way?
When whiskey and blood run together
Did you hear anyone pray?

        Roy Acuff

death the companion at the wheel revolving as ever

his priceless smile his bejeweled fingers his askance

and daily glance over his shoulder to certify the wounded

who will not rise again and lofty his words soundless

orient of mantra-syllables the defiant polish of his skin

hands immaculate as razors with the power to make

the heavens invisible forever and foot on the gas speeding

up to a million light years a minute thrills with peals

of laughter the inchoate noise of the cosmos coming to

terms with itself beneath a banyan tree in the fetid

Gangetic plains a grammar a textbook illusion a faded

painting of the Lord-of-the-Universe dancing on the tip

of the original vowel in the shape of a water-born lotus

immense as night and twice as silent and comrade death

staring intently ahead to a road-block unable to avert

the inevitable crash to smithereens—*Buddhas !* tenfold

at the crossroads prepared to count the uncountable

metal and bone and grass the track of blood sinuous

like a thin cloud of gas zigzagging across consciousness

and alcohol blooming gorgeous as a thousand sunsets

mirage of adolescence and love ! nothing is ever reversed

nor made redundant in the rear-view mirror

birth is but an innovation and breath but a rumor

the great error is in seeing ! whispers *little-brother-death*

atavistic untruths the chariot upside down in the ditch

keeps spinning and the mangled but magnificent steeds

the gift of Dawn's one bright hour in dewfall stare

impotently into the stardust of unnumbered asterisks

still glowing in the burning water of memory

how much motion there was in the finger lost in grass

everything that ever was and growing up and grief !

things that linger dwindling in the smoking atmospheres

architecture of heat and the resounding echo of stone

coming to be and going out of existence in a trice--

outside of the concept of gravity and the weight of

a single photograph what else can matter ?

01-30-22

FOR MAX WHO IS EVERYWHERE ABSENT

limited memory of fruit ripening in a season
gone astray monthless epochs days without number
designations for sky and clouds in unknown languages
to understand was to be baffled to taste the rinds
and to discard the petals and stalks and bewildered
counting on one hand the essence of poetry enumerating

glyphs and vowels and consonant clusters in graphs
depicted on cyclopean walls mnemonic structures
to no avail what was forgotten was the ability to see
correctly what originates in sleep seeking daylight
but gets lost along the way and the shadowy realms
of extended distance and longing the dark woods
voices from other realms logarithms and x-rays
a child with both feet gone numb and a bridge
a route not to be taken and hills of smoke and rue
strangers at a pass exchanging masks futilities and
absences the requirements for entrance to Hades
located beside the abandoned gasoline pumps near
the winter of the great specters of quick succession
speech modification and lamps revolving high in
the luster of the moon's shivered hues invisible
as horses in a Scotland left to the imagination
cairns and cliffs and faces painted eerily blue eleven
times softer than the whispered intaglio that takes
the ears to a sea of regret and pentimento and
the small stone elevation a challenge to the comatose
! sparks and detonations of heat and always the
inarticulate envelope containing the shorn hair
memento of ten years spent in the *other* world
! wherever the solar car travels whether on streets
or ditched in embankments of sorrow and grief
the half-lit alphabets of noon and its forgeries
fail at spelling out the full name and birth register
only the afterlife of certificates denoting demise

and expulsion from the kingdom of leaf and branch

backyards of the playful kick and jump toward flight

! if only the paper wings attached to the shoulders

had not burned so quickly

01-31-22

JE LANGUIS D'AMÈRE MORT

there was a side to Joe that dug Frank Sinatra

accompanied by the Nelson Riddle Orchestra

though he preferred Billie Holiday's *God Bless the Child*

music that transported him in his student-marijuana stupor

to other climes to unimaginable futures of prophecy and deceit

when did all this happen//where did it all go ?

up in a puff of the tarot cigarette passed around

in cellar rooms stifled with jazz-horn imagery

French impressionist acrylics cloud-shifts orange poison

blooms altering the sky by half a hemisphere and

at large the revolving faces of girlfriends wives illusory

mistresses the summer the fish went belly up

in Lake Michigan's corrosive waters and distances

of silvery planet Zavuya with its pyramids and surf

and ageless adolescents who would accompany Joe

into some dream-spell reality flying airplanes

over *jungles wet with rain* and song-birds like Etta James
or Jo Stafford plugged in his ear drifting off into
the big sleep on the other side of death which he could
foresee and kept predicting donning his white prophet
raiment glowing words mingling scat-singing with religion
stolen Tibetan colors spinning on a vast mandala
wheel all his own a universe followed by other universes
even as he found himself walking home late afternoons
through a park littered with childhood references
to Xochimilco and Chapultepec covered with sun-dust
the busy emporium of ideas beneath Teotihuacan's
ahistorical geometries and the immense redundancies of space
in the orient of an LSD trip or magnums of powerful booze
head upside down in a sling somewhere in archaic Greece
rock and grass and meandering waters of the Zumbro
the New World Symphony echoing in springtime breeze
dragonflies and innocence wafting between ecstasy
and its unconscious twin *light* – re-created pasts !
alcohol and nights without cognition speed and dizzy
unrelenting flights to Ulan Bator or Brasilia until
it all caught up the jingo and buttress of philosophies
metaphysical scams at his bejeweled fingertips
in the *Wee small hours of the morning* when drugged voices
return to haunt the staggered mind in an attempt to recapture
some essence held within *the* instant of recognition
when all of space and time are re-worked in a cerebral

cyclotron and the various music the flitting melody

die and die again beside a resemblance to Mom

in her floral-patterned tuberculosis dress of relativity

always the last thing remembered in the long spiral

downward through the *selva oscura* to southland

where the blues masters perform their delta classics

My love will never die ! I'm a King Bee !

on an eerie radio program beamed from the Mayo clinic

it is never anywhere it is always nowhere

the lost cinema about twins in the Sierra Madre

being born going astray listening always listening

to the last song ever recorded *You belong to me*

02-01-22

ARCHAEOLOGY OF THE SOUL

in the first place the streets don't go anywhere

a resemblance to long abandoned islands

vineyards overgrown with dust embolisms

worm and cricket have their day in lost furrows

brothers joined hands near the battered tree-trunk

dryads and nymphs fauns satyrs the whole lot

used to play by these rusted wrecks gateway of kings

the once and never futility of trying to read

let alone puzzling over these scratches on copper-plate
urns the dimensions of a human filled with oblivion
histories of rain and the tides moon-struck darkening
isolated places where the solar homophone is loud
distance and the effort to survive and testaments
of skin and bone the obdurate struggle for light
willing obsolescence in the lists of dynasties
and speech ! hills and woods and rolling twilight lands
distinctions are never made between the first
and the last letters of a word and the noise and riot
welling up from the maps of undiscovered cities
chariots that rock back and forth Pluto at the helm
and the whitening shadows of Persephone and
sheldrake and kestrel and soaring kite bearing
messages from afar the signal to depart !
stasis and motion circle and linearity constantly
inconstant in a bed of retrograde sleep amorphous
as shapes tend to be in the dream inside the dream
where names foment their own pronominal disasters
metrics and realities of stone and grass
alignment of the houses of the zodiac at noon
when silence is unbearably deafening
can the ear maintain its hold on the echoes
emanating from the small pink shell of memory ?
digging even deeper below the rock foundations
fossil ideas membrane of thoughts the mind's outcast

wanderings meandering through dry-beds of the Nile

specters of pyramids and the wind-eaten face of the sphinx

oracular conjunctions vowels abracadabra recitation

redundancies of crossroads and midnights

resolution to stop moving to keep to the shadows

where recollection of the body is untenable

texts without sounds ! consonants strung out

in long chronologies of vacated lamps and ignition

in its own drop-box vain excess of pronunciation

the unsettled gift of consciousness !

enigma and foothold the miasma of truth

waters receding from the flood before time

masses of unshaped continents emerging from

the single alpha and never anywhere in sight

a place to lay the unbidden head and to close the eyes

to vision to be free at last from the legibility

of prescriptions and x-rays and anatomy lessons

outline and definition of the sublime *One*

dissolved in the ecstatic shapelessness of eternity

02-02-22

THE BEDROOM WITHOUT BORDERS

the last place first beginning with insomnia

the zero effect of darkness on the lapsing mind

visionary ciphers retrograde drill of the hours

a childhood up front lawns of distant innocence

it could have been *other* the release of light

from its origins language of formations and

badly lit thoughts relentless implosion of sound

the ever changing habit of mind to renew its

cells as if to make another world come daylight

storm of leaves and birds lifting off carrying

still another soul into the empyrean that exists

beyond the visible sky's infinite azure lexicon

a tributary runs beneath it a chaos of umbrellas

grief's geometries and extended rain clouds

keep your Russia your small-pox and affidavits !

the left-wing of death is beating fast the pulse

of a nation without statehood the far reaches

beyond night's unknown limits a contusion

the eternal inch of consciousness that forgets !

memory's lost hemisphere emerging from

the non-existent lotus of Brahma and horizons

tilting just beyond the eyelid's dumb periphery

angels and salamanders exchanging colors falling

between the interstices of an Etruscan painting

Pluto and Hermes and the maiden of Despair

plant-life submerged in the dialect of matter

least expected the dead *pharaoh* of infinity

louder than the last time he approached the Wall

bangs his insolent fists against the silent syllable

that defines how far a deity's alphabet can go

fusion and fission fugue and ornamental spot

red and black green and yellow the path down

to the Peninsula of resurrected tyrannicides

ruins opaque shifts of destiny phonetic decay

imitations of ink redundant and terrifying

because the door won't open nor the vowel

all the numbers have been counted but for

one slight blade of grass darkening and slender

on the edge of time that contains the epic noise

which is the numberless sequences of lives

like planets diminished since the dawn of space

subtracted between now and tomorrow morning

punctuations and nothing more of oblivion

02-03-22

ULYSSES MUSING ON THE PASSAGE HOME

to tire of memory feel the weight pulling

down toward some mental Sargasso dense

irrevocable with lost images petrified thoughts

a lingering sense of eternity's disposed instant

floating on the turgid surface and do mariners

who hail from Ithaca still wave through eons

of mnemonic waste longing to be freed from Circe's

bewitching transformations everything is obsession

and detail redundancies of a poetic meter hues

fading on a funeral urn depicting the descent

to Hades of Achilles head first into the warning

black syllable of the underground sun a tender

if nothing else evocation a remnant of lyric

words cut off before completion and sounds

the ear strains to remember in its narcotic quandary

whether to emit light-signals or simply remain

as a fossil embedded in cyclopean rock a formation

of noise isolated from the origins of space such

as memory is a dedication to revolving ecstasies

and despond reiterated catastrophes in grass

the distances of all remembrance pale and indistinct

in hills where dialects of remote grammars dissolve

a fist raised to the tributary skies of Thursday or

the eventuality of a twilit porch with paper lanterns

the whir of invisible wings the fixed eyes of fireflies

glowing in the dance and if only and if only

the mind retaliates with a repeated dream of life

each of us taking a hand to help shape the air

that winnows around the perfumed skin and hair

of an evanescent partner a swoon a migration

of the nerve to lunar hospices where reflections

in opaque glass remind us of a stringent mortality

that though the gods move among us like shadows

vibrating against heated concrete they have

nothing to do with us figments of *their* imagination

poetry and delusion license to shift unseen from

generation to generation mourning each passing

moment of breath even as oncoming night

takes us by the knees and we fail at arriving

at the still-point where leaves perfect their silence

maze and loom of galaxies buried in time

02-04-22

THE ADVANCE OF CIVILIZATION

must we read more of these books ?

we have cleared the land and given

names to exotic plants and yet and yet

the sky lies fallow beneath our feet and
clouds enormous with sleep anchor themselves
by the distance it takes to reach noon and
once there and making treaties with statues
and guessing by the darkening plight of the sun
how little remains nevertheless we forge ahead
into still another hour being with a woman
whose mysterious appearance at the reading
of the oracular syllables disturbs more than
it comforts for hers is a shadow lengthening
by the minute and turning her words into
lyrical apogees she becomes more infirm
an endeavor to multiply without increase and
a finger of rain a cloister of breath some brief sounds
the worm is in the eye ! how can we hear so much
without listening beforehand what the rocks
have to say and the gravel which is the position of night
even as we lose our way in the dense wood and
seeking direction only go in circles asking the self
if the small deer at the margin were a sign
can there be histories without chronology ?
somewhere in the middle is a path of light
voices murmuring in the underbrush surrender
their meaning to the great diapason of air
among us there are many who cannot stop grieving
the satellites that abound as mistakes plummeting

in the heavens are conjectures and abstractions

of a recollection of a morning filled with promises

Stop ! the illustrated gazetteers were wrong

there are no latitudes or longitudes only seas

boundless and puzzling that storm the ear

and toward the south where the dead travel

disconfigured and diminished by their own repetitions

that is where we are bound without compass

in the little light of a single match-flare and without

purpose the burden of memorizing hills and mounds

and the stark complaint of ants both red and black :

had we but wings !

02-05-22

WAITING FOR DAYLIGHT

para Arturo Mantecón

even if I am not myself volcanic ash

debris from former deaths not anticipated

island adrift between two mountains

each darker than the other and moving

ever so slowly through silent cataracts of sound

distances to no avail between the space

of this universe and the immobility of the next

lying in wait with lynx eyes beside beds of poetry
not yet written excavations of cuneiform fossils
resonating speech from the second millennium BCE
sunrise of all matter and divided into syllables
and noises of rock and gravel and wheels
of great invisible chariots driven by gods
of cloud and rain and the tiny vowels of grief
sorrowing for the one who disappeared last Wednesday
nor is it clear that I am having these thoughts
a section of the galaxies that circulate in the veins
for me to wake ! the diphthongs and lairs
where dichotomies persist of being and non-being
consciousness of the leaf ! everything is running
toward a dry river bed in search of the reflections
souls emit ascending from the body's hemispheres
and outside on the street a hooded entity
nameless and threatening awaits in his automobile
a vision of purely electric origin ! hands occur and
grasses and the formidable twilights of history
when nation states surrender their craving and
succumb to the nymphs who dwell in mirrors and combs
the wet parallaxes of a divine intuition feminine and
wildly red and bright which is a sign of the oncoming day
and should I proceed from this membrane and delusion
should I exit this corporeal realm and approach
the fire-altars attended by the sacred vultures

then will the full extent of time manifest !

bones and texts and scriptures none will ever read

and the few numbers that matter which

are the sum of a life and its limitation of breath

where is this place I inhabit this mind

this corrupt division of phonetics and amnesia ?

daybreak ! the infinite and multiple sky of light !

02-06-22

"CIECO NUME, SPIRITO SPIETATO"

para mi hermano José

after the light comes regret broken music

rising from a forgotten summer's dusty fields

free-song of cicadas like the rumors of tragedy

in a Greek chorus played out on shattered marble

steps that cling to reverberations echoes of a sea

long turned to stone in the ear's hemisphere of doubt

does anyone ever remember the beginnings ?

things are always in their midst somewhere between

the rains of an unasked for month and the heat

that repeats its cycles mercilessly in windows

that are the afterthought of memory looking out

on the storm-tossed grass and trees evocations

of a language no one recalls hearing but the statues

whose eternal noon is a torment of aphasia and grief

to have been born ! always the paradigm of loss

beforehand the recognition of the second day's brief

register before night with its stuttering asterisks

of poignant distance resumes its unfolding dichotomies

we were here once ! we played the truant and beggar

we roamed the streets' skeletal maps knowing

we would do this only once before plunging

like unheralded planets of black homophones

into the relentless waters that took Achilles

and so many other high-school graduates who

persist if that as fading photographs hieratic

effigies ephemeral shadows sketched in darkness

02-07-22

BLANK VISCERA

the tragedian's instructions call for a sky

that cannot be renovated on a canvas surface

and voices of echolalia the babble infesting

the elocution of deities who have lost control

affairs are not human but preternatural

speech and longevity of breath are not givens
but the fragile donations of Minerva who has
gone stark raving mad in this epoch of illness
and overwhelming untruths and wherever one
steps the miasma and morass of an unfinished
fifth act tarnish the expectation of applause
infirmities of the soul ! who has the eyes to see
beyond what words cannot describe the vast
anodyne reaches of space untrammeled by thought ?
the cast of characters the personae and stage
are but painted nouns ascribed to a faulty memory
dim and sketchy recollections of doomed kings
of servants run amok of queens blinded by
lust and tenderness of early deaths and unwanted
births the whole panoply of mortal regrets
falling in love and hate and hands lopped off
for what they have recorded vowels shifted out
of place punctuations and affidavits and laws
blurring emotions and misrepresentations hues
of dialect and innuendo the ennui of afternoons
one is forced to relive despite medical advice and
in a word bedlam and manicomio doubles of the *other*
twins and profligates wining in the scullery with
debauched nursemaids the handsome likeness of horse
and rider racing to a common doom and shouts
the ever present noise of the brain ! blank viscera

spilling out of an unwritten script and the sleep

of Momus triumphant exegesis of the archaic

when leaf and foment silence and penance

are all to no avail in this destroyed work

02-07-22

POEMA HUMANO

all-mothering air ! I fling my poetry books at you

no confusion like the sounds that do not match

the billions of stars that are unspellable words

this is neither the first nor the last breath

no more than oxygen that operates mysteriously

to keep us alive is fixed and tangible and there

are hosts of declensions and conjugations at work

in the mind's unbearable grammar that keeps us

rattled and somehow moving across the mutable

terrain of consciousness which is nothing but noise

audible junk the hesitation between being and light

the insufferable moment of birth reckless annotations

and speech-acts of statuary blind in noontime's

harrowing mirror when the sun's ominous passage

destroys all previous events and moments

leaving us with deranged hands empty eyes ears

collapsed into echoes of stone and gravel

monstrous climates of sleep ! how to wake from

this dream of blood and solitude and to recall

without wishing to the islands and the sirens

and the multiple child who transfigured a coma

into space-flight and the eventualities of death

among the lesser entities the grasses and covens

where darkness lies in wait for broken toys

how long is the inch of eternity ? the fuse

and fossil embedded in the transient winds

when least expected everything comes to a head

a violent but unheard syllable archaic as the oceans

is the translation to heaven a language in itself ?

salvation and revival penance and grieving

all-mothering air ! I fling my poetry books at you

02-08-22

OTRO POEMA HUMANO

eco-systems fade love songs go on and on

mind fades into a parenthesis of doubt and longing

problems of experience and memory

amnesia and ambition futile gestures in

Sunday afternoon's terrible ennui

hands recall paths not taken fingers go trembling

lost in the darker grasses of last Thursday

when the morgue received the soul's castoff husk

brown and exhausted like a cicada's

a symphony is an agreement an observation

made by winged insects and by leaves shaken

from the ear of the wind in the pallor

of a late night sky when stars disintegrate

turning into pollen yellow as a lunar ellipse

while here between the two frozen poles and

the unmitigated arousal of the many waters

drowned reflections captured in the sun's

vast immobile eye seem to direct the heavens

toward some vain disappearance west of the hills

where philosophy and urgency linger some small poems

mostly in *dolce stil novo* but then what matter

the rain the illicit fogs mourning the loss of

distance and it is still moving the exquisite

sense of the hours shifting as shadows

without inheritance across the vague dominion

where dreams turn to sand and dawn starts

up like a startled horse racing the empty field

of time such as imagination is halt and start

a few words bringing the world to an end

sound tumbling out of a sunflower's harmony

alcohol beyond blessing ! and this perfect day

no reckoning but azure infinities & polygraphs
everything so ineffably beautiful I cannot contain
myself and without knowing why weep aloud
so many smitten syllables ! the past erased
repeatedly by the nymphs of invisibility
why am I so alone and empty !

02-09-22

THE FAINT RESURRECTION OF TIME

pockets and combs and small pieces of
colored glass that tell when the next absence
will be when the following hour will strike
seems to remember nothing to recall only
the weather was stormy purple thunderclouds
overhead grass darkening like night walking
as we were home suspicious of distance looming
with its derelict hills of another realm white
and apple-green the slope the stucco walls
erected suddenly in front and the cemetery
of automobile parts the shining rainbow
splotches of oil on the concrete would a finger
learn to erase or a fist to lower like a derrick
the surface of sound and the errant path
of air blowing memory off course wildly

silent as if windows and passages through mud
or snow could seasons matter would there
really be a ceremony for the newly dead
the church of empty wood and tiny engravings
that stood for saints echoing marble shafts
the mind in its unsettled motion to order
if it only could speech into patterns of sense
meaning the world would manifest reflected
in horizons of tarnished color schemes or
the highway with its promise of big cities
would get us somewhere else would let us
feel other than we really were a radio and ear
a fossil in the dirt and removing shadows
what else could the sky offer descending
and the house emerging from a furrow deep
in the park's ornamental hell where sleep
and the orient of a ringing bell so remote
lay our heads on resonating stone dreaming
the faint resurrection of time was at hand

02-09-22

BURNING MILESTONE SUTRA

for Miriam Tarcov on her 79th birthday

let us take this lawn and spread it out

and little hills and sudden lakes that mirror

the mind's small craft of speech and design

what art so plentiful a wheel of colors

and mastery of hand and drawing fields

far and wide the quest for mystery and tombs

highways that round the unknown or paths

and derelict deer that nibble in the brush

a Buddha big as granite and silent as a sphere

of sky seems to appear and oracles of light

the distance of a recent past or a life yet

to live and phrases recondite that are years

how many is a number none can ken like

the ciphers revolving in the Buddha's hand

and rock and grass and the multiple infinite

of water feminine as all matter is and ether

and fire and pinnacles of sound the unheard

note of a music vast as the desert in the eye

troubles too come and go and words printed

in *italics* that have no sense and brighter

still the trembling suns as many as a trillion

that vanish like the wind but what can compare

to the tiny illustration you bear beneath sleep's

opaque mirror *Vajradhatu* white eight-armed

the lightning that bears rosary and arrow

illumination without death the furious light
that precedes birth and grief and sorrow too
the way is littered and shards of glass like
vows in the purpose to *become* yet alone
despite the massive mandala of the universe
you persist illusion dream and memory
the choice of a single life the spear-head
that is nothing more than a house of sand
within the illustration woven into your face
of a radiance meteoric and instantaneous :
your passage through the noise of time
your presence in the absence of the known
diamond realm and womb of future lands
today ! burning milestone of another year !

02-10-22

REFLECTIONS ON VANISHING TIME

after all these years filtered occasionally with light
prevails ominous and all-extending darkness a night
of boundless invention studded with disappearing asterisks
my life ! one cries when the day still lacks hours and
only the evasive dream of memory haunting illustration
of shadows grass and wooden fences punctuating
the distant shout of a childhood in hills of absence and

longing to have understood just once the density of air

the still-point when breath converges with a music

of silence and aphasia when language is loss and

repetitions of rock and echo are the stagecraft of illusion

harbors and lakes smaller divergences of water multiple

and always beyond touch the reach of thought but

a fleet of clouds scudding low on a deathless autumn day

it was nothing but a cinema reel a fiction of passing sights

mountains that come and go ! houses afloat in the ether

of archaic redundancies myth and fragment of wind

trees-of-life in dialogue with the unfinished statues of noon

when the unrelenting sun black-spot of oblivion is equidistant

between the origin and the diminishment of the cosmos

moments of bilateral noise and supremacy of gravity

everything revolving around itself both stasis and motion

the famous but only half-recalled verses of the oracle

uttered by an unknown voice hidden in stone and gravel

when homecoming and nostalgia flood the soul with

dimensions of space and instamatic reconditioning

once-and-only minute--eternity ! where are we now ?

02-10-22

AN EVENING IN THE BALKANS

"Și inima aceea, ce geme de durere
Și sufletul acela, ce cîntă amorțit"

      Mihai Eminescu, Din străinătate

the broken carriage wheel why I stopped
to spend the remnant of time in the Carpathians
does anyone speak these tongues without a history ?
a poetry of dead summers of stone and granite
that open with a magic vowel and peaks
too high to see too lofty to reconsider
an archaic owl Minerva's ghost hovers
in the map of tangled and bare branches
and after so many years traveling from dialect
to dialect I don't know where my mind is
nor why Apollo instructed me if it was only
illusion and not an oracle that was uttered
during a noon of marble and false enquiry
light is only a summary account of time !
what matters is the morning after when
the orient is disclosed in its page of ornamental
sounds and noises bric-a-brac jabber of mantra
and trance the broken syllables that end before
they begin the headache and trauma of memory
going over the same details splitting rock-
formations speaking to the dead in their
ominous invisibility trying to identify objects
in space prior to falling asleep the enormous

dream of a double identity of a shadow
in the mirror of the combs and threads and
essential grasses that bring the dark to a close
fruition of the moon ! looking out from the balcony
over the sheepcotes and wells of this ancient
Roman province it all comes back to me
the book and the ivory-handled wheel barrow
the intransigent consonants interspersed
between leaf and vine and the trees that suffer
for having learned to listen to rumors in the wind
the ear ! the fuse and detonation of a small spot
misplaced items in lost luggage the horses
who have become human overnight and
their language back and forth the sameness
and loss of discipline of Latin grammar
yes and no ! to have come this far deceived
by Apollo and Minerva whose crystalline ovations
are meant for someone else and alone
with grief I shed distinctions of mask and
persona knowing I have never been myself
but a sequence of strange ramblings
punctuation and disorder of a scrapbook
torn photographs of the nameless with whom
I graduated in the century of the atomic blast
and then returns to me a girl *that* goddess
who was *she*? what was her sorrow ?
02-11-22

CHARADES

in whose memory do we exist ?

in whose dream are we the mysterious strangers ?

are we the prey of celestial nymphs or demons ?

added years do not make for wisdom

with age we only become enigmas of ourselves

to a mystery we were born to a greater mystery

we tend our ever faltering steps and fade

into the secret that lies on the other side of breath

light is nothing but shadow of the dark

do we sleep inside someone else's sleep ?

what is the shape and size of the air that holds us

bound to this hypnotic and ceaseless rhythm ?

do our hands know who we truly are or

are they blindly seeking to possess the *other*?

sounds come and go through the ear's dumb labyrinth

noises and crepuscular echoes the pale composition

of a music which is all distance and longing

heard only once in the phantom era between births

what is human life but stages in phonetic development

small breakdowns between syllabic sequences

in which dictionary are we only lexical units ?

language at best is the expression of something lost

remote hesitation and stuttering aphasia and amnesia

that plague total recall of innocence

we fade we pale we vanish ere night takes us

first the ankles then by the knees and we tumble

out of a mirror into the profundities of outer space

hypnotized asterisks of so many untold histories

can you see me ? am I plural or infinite or merely singular

a thought moving abstract and illusory through mind's

insane image of a conjectured universe

great and feminine waters plunge from the skies

gravity and stasis and lunar divisions that govern

emotions and the tides of tragedy and renunciation

a level at a time and you come into focus dim outline

on a photographic plate the visualized shout

of surprise and dismay of cognition

and looking about we see the *others* the ones

who have been sundered from the whole dressed

in pronoun and mask like us and so we become confused

picture-show figurines playing a game of charades

imperfect silhouettes of adolescence and dying

02-12-22

RECOGNIZING ME FOR WHAT I AM

say farewell to the old body the adolescent one

gone four hundred sutures ago a threnody of

withering skin parchment for eyelids the excess

gravity of an extra year and fondly drowning

in memories of a pool the size of the southern

hemisphere where the body plunged out of the sky

into the placid waters to swim above and below

Neptune's mystical surfaces a hand waving to

the biosphere and the airs governed by Zeus

polyvalent accented billowing grace of existence

for a moment only as if for once the Greek meaning

to the sounds that paraded in the air the solemnities

of standing on the porch roof demanding attention

the positive unfolding of language sensuously prompt

was ripe for decay like the uncountable seconds

spent in the fields with love-eternal in her lithe

unknowing shape yielding to the forms of sweat

to the pallor and cycle of heat and to the embrace

how swift it all goes in a trice the horses that

raced the clouds and the bottomlands where

lying in wait Pluto prepares the annual exit

for an unwitting Persephone or doomed Achilles

that was who we were ! unfathomable darkness

emerging from cavernous insect labyrinths where

we lay our bodies down to read the unconscious

text of an innumerable and impossible future

you and me ! secrets that devoured the ear with

insane pledges and rumors of infinity in an hour

and night ! the thousand-eyed temple of enormity

to which we dedicated those bodies ominous

with an afterbirth of sorrow and intoxication

farewell to virgin ambitions of unwritten poems

to the skill-set of ignorance and denial to *youth*

which is the glorious cloister of dust and death !

02-13-22

SAINT VALENTINE'S DAY SUTRA

when pleasure becomes purely phonetic

the beauties of the world become an open wound

and to mistake day's brief light for eternity !

spoken words are not intended to be part of the dialogue

between the soul and its invisible and absent mate

the primeval sound echoing in the stone like

the rush of water from some unseen but feminine source

the rumor of leaves trespassing silence in search

of an oracle that will explain the inability of the future

to ever manifest and the constant buoying of air

transcendental and migratory as a flight of birds

soaring into the sun's intimate and black homophone

what ! the innumerable complaints of love

the triangles and ciphers and whizzing darts all

laying claim to the heart's mortal enigma

to what aim the embrace and the kiss and separation

the nightfall of emotions and the hesitation as ever

of the sea to come rushing on its knees to plead

the cause of time and gravity and flood the fields

of distance and take each mountain as it comes

and trace with tears the outline of the *beloved*

we all come to the faltering steps of memory

puzzled that life has come and gone and birth was

only the foreshadowing of death the invincible *lover*

what are the unheard sounds the notes heralded as unique

in the enormous revolving cosmos that cannot be defined ?

come let is surrender the body's illusory climax

the hair that binds the wind in sheaves the hands

whose purpose is to look for what can never be

anti-matter negative film corrosive lunar destinies

whatever it is the path *is* the error and the noise

the infinite disorder and calamity where the body dwells

one minute the fixed copula and the next the storm

that reduces everything to gravel and grains of sand

'tis love ! the poets shout with disheveled glee

troubadours and mounts and damsels in their towers

locked in promises of everlasting bliss !

'tis love that makes the world a drum of sound

and brings the skies to a sudden halt and turns each

word into its opposite so nothing is ever understood

for such have we come to be in one another a self

that has no shadow a mirror without reflection

the one and only One dissolved in its plurality

02-14-22

THE MUSIC OF THE SPHERES

the full body of knowledge and literature

loss and lack and longing inadvertent redundancies

resonance of the soul's sea of inner turmoil

the ear in its shattered labyrinthine composure

fond memories of the leaf and the triangle of sky

the smaller lessons of grass and dew and hill-slopes

winter and its deviant chills and blossoming beneath

snow-banks color and hue the yellows and purples

fingering their way through attitudes of air like

a music meant to remain in its nascent unheard stage

a reckoning of sounds and articulations the mind's

primordial myths bittersweet and kinetic trying

to move beyond the cliffs of sleep and darkness

to whatever moment of day most resembles eternity

a childhood away and fragments isolated from

the greater script of being and becoming the ledger

of uncounted lives ciphers poignant and tender

mythologies distant and archaic lesions and wounds

spears that split the winds in half and cries incarnate
that evoke the written word centuries later and
fuse and fission the disclosures of thought reckless
ambivalence of breath and the careers of dying
unto the moment of recognition and regret –
state of affairs known as *ashes* or graduation day
when bodies learn to depart sorrowing as statues
relieved of their shadows lifting their mute cries
to gods who have no right to be and irreversibility
what little Greek was imparted and philosophies
of the atom and its omega flux and dissolution
the bedlam of spatial magma coming into sight
and reverting matter to its essential chaos
visions ! the infinite decibel that divides hemispheres
and grief at the root because the one can never
really get to know the *other* a life of imperfections
buying and selling books leaving most everything
half-read misinterpreted or merely ignored
comes the day of mortal reckoning the scales
tilted toward the side of disrepute and error
the symphonic works that were never composed
resounding in the massive and silent sands
that rush through rumors of immortality
a universe of unmatched coordinates in suspense
to lay the puzzled head down on its still-point
stone and ethereal punctuations *oblivion*

02-15-22

A DAY IN AN ADOLESCENT AFTERNOON

for bob ness, slade schuster and james balfour

concerning the next life rounding out memory

sections of air collapsed cloud-murals paint

chipping off nails whole monuments of atmosphere

toppled by a winsome breath hair out of place

youth at a gallop out of the gym into the library

fractions and iotas and figments and fading hues

a hand two fingers a signal aimed at the Mayo clinic

disposable thoughts turning the corner where the wind

gestates its ensuing tempest of unheard syllables

book-plates music lessons across town bad piano

learning descant and overture and the solemnities

of "going steady" in the drug store's cheap perfumes

Christ was not born today nor Apollo his winged shafts

did Achilles fell nor do other heroic names claim

a place in the afternoon's gravity gazing through

chains of smoke and winter's brooding symphonies

what will it be like when I die what will the music be ?

hiding between the covers of a book dismissing geometry

the Friday night sports event the multiple wounds

of alcohol in the blood imagination run wild

with a poem sure to win the contest delivered

in 16th century Elizabethan drawl and the guffaws

and clicks and snorts and grunts plate glass windows

shatter and a snare drum with its handsome soul

as always out of place the long darkening line
of ennui and trance when can it ever end this
foreboding of highways going east and diesel fuel
fragrant in the future season and trees bowing to
an infernal home-town deity who governs nights
and rivers and longing the aspersions of love
"breaking up" tossing the dime-store ring into a ditch
starting an engine that has nowhere to go but
the radio capturing songs a thousand miles away
isn't that what it's all about ?
will it take eight decades to realize the futility ?

02-16-22

THE DISTANT REGARD OF THE GODS

today's awakening is just that a glimmer
of light among the pebbles of consciousness
striving to recall last night's dreams a song
intimations of hostility an almost Egyptian
hypnosis shielding details of unwanted thoughts
a radio of rumors lyrics of wanton dereliction
resonance and error as usual the mind what it
cannot finish and eyes to see what the dark
envelopes a cry of memory to loosen the sheets

from their lunatic folds to lift first one finger

then the whole hand and mirror in the small

cavities the multiple failures at perfecting

the leaf's primordial outline a grief in hills

abandoned by the sun and wary that north

is a direction taking steps to correct division

of the hemispheres between past and present

the sudden remembrance of pertinent deaths

month and date minute and hour the telephone

and from afar the collapsed breathing-machines

reported like galactic messages that nothing

and no one can be revived even if daylight

sends a warrant to the door-post and hazard

and redundancy sway the judges who sit high

in their Olympian pedestals rendering futile

and evasive arguments for the death-penalty

a god suddenly manifests in his little shining

holding a buckler and something metallic

a sorrowing treble in his voice like a bird wounded

in flight and leaning over to take another shadow

back to the skies bids farewell with a glance

that in itself is both beautiful and murderous

how long this day is a possibility who can tell

02-17-22

THE SUMMER OF 1978

the impossibility of recovering the glass

let alone the reflections it once captured

what can a dictionary tell us of that accident ?

faltering minds data at a loss for explanation

the moment the plane lifted off with the stretcher

bearing the amnesia victim and the skies parted

the nebulous distinctions between left and wrong

and cloud bustle and infamy of breath on earth

the human plight of memory and identity longing

and confusion the meanings of words suddenly

frayed missing absent puzzling conjectures

of sound and distance questions of pronoun

and place the motion to depart while standing still

on a marble pedestal like the monument of a god

stubbornly mutilated and blinded by the airs that swallow

shadows in the brilliant childhood noon when

megalithic effigies of eternity waver like mirages

in the non-existent water that floods vision

or is it merely the instant after the great solar

homophone explodes silently in the reverberation

and chorus of hidden insects drowning the ear

so much of that summer's intense remoteness

the vestiges of greenery and ivy the crawling walls

of stucco and derangement the phonetic decay

evident in every stuttering syllable employed

by the brain in an effort to reconstruct the persona

experiencing language and its derelict intentions

what a hemorrhage of thought ! life's abracadabra

piecing together the patch-work quilt of boyhood

labyrinthine intricacies of inoperable grammar

how to separate the vacations in India and Morocco

from the sudden fever and crippling illness ?

what remains ? the future of ash predicted

by the Turkish doctor who promised quality of life

the surgical nuisance of experience playing on

a tightrope extended over the Milky Way and

prepared to snap at the least random vowel

suddenly dislocated in the variable pronunciation

of medical prescriptions and Homeric epic

oracular and coded messages of grief

echoes of plastic toys forgotten in the corner

left to darken in the imagined space-flight

of the boy for whom that June was forever

Max

02-18-22

MORE DEATHS THAN ONE

like bees enraged at the onslaught of winter

or ants looking for ancient cities in the soil

the mind goes through the rutilating galaxies

in search of the pure space of non-being

just so the soul dissolves in rivers of ink

blind majesties of moon and marble seeking

the mirror's endless night in passageways

of sleep and memory dreams fraught with

untold and unwanted images of grief

encountered along the way through woods

solemn as unfinished cathedrals ruins of thought

language that has no purpose among sounds

and the vast and unformed content of air

both breath-giving and pointless gathering

shapes of leaf and rock and smothering grass

with its epicycles of heat or cold invisibilities

ponder the enigma that we can never know

what comes of the millions of unrecorded decibels

in our puerile concept of history and time

unreckoned instants of a multiple unity

that all life is a deviation from a silent stasis

the sheath of darkness that surrounds light

incorruptible and chaotic divisions without

origin unfathomable punctuations between

the immense syllables of an unknown whim

atavistic etymology of anti-matter exploding

in the depthless ear of stone that yearns for gravity

and what of the afternoon of blazing love ?

like statues imploring the deities of smoke

and pulp for a moment of consciousness

when identities were exchanged and mouths

played flutes and hair and combs and wax

impressions of the great emotions of poetry

how slight the inflexion of the verb *to be* !

chairs of pronouns playing games of chance

and to die and keep dying the second death

the one that puts a firm imprint on the winds

listening as ever for the phantom seas that

come rushing to take us by the knees

surprise ! that brief eternity of cognition

boomerang and tension – redundancies

buried in the archaic sands of the Lethe

02-19-22

THE POEM ABOUT POETRY REVISED

for Indran Amirthanayagam

last things end first listening intently afternoons
as they whisper out of voice the library's least
corner a shelf out of reach decimal points away
from the alphabet and splendors too of glorious
pedigrees monarchs and divans and empurpled
Byzantine sunsets thrones of light and lattice clouds
echoes of matter the heavens on a page illustrating
the vowels of celestial formation dusky winged
angels singing voiceless praises to the deities
of unborn verse genius and relic of scriptures
unlicensed version totem redundancies surreal
and automatic as I am penning these larval
phrases textual innovations of the epic device
summoned by muses nine the intransigence of
breathing and the feminine waters of inspiration
linking thought to throttle the engines of mind
such as beauties out of sequence walls unfolding
depth and gravity of the just glimpsed face of
one whose ethereal presence is leaf and memento
a statue of air and nothing more the abyss and
ditch of memory whence all present tenses derive
the illusion to proceed trading pronouns and gloves
the drugs that enlighten love the heights of sound

wordlessly chaotic a hymn without references
a counter-balance to the sands and ink-stones
of writing come midnight and pouring incense
of imagination through the sign for seduction
head and gravel point of delivery swooning steam
of sleep and devoured by the minute asterisks
that dwell below the surface of Aphrodite's skin
a luscious collapse of the senses and giving no
more than the tongue can in its envelope of grace
portents of evening hills of dialect and imitation
resonance in *italics* asleep enumerating the moons
that circle so languidly the heat of a missing summer
like the time we lost ourselves in fields of maize
when the coppery sun reverberated its homophone
so loud all we could hear was a brace of consonants
evaporating in the windy labyrinth of Aeolus
drowsy sepulchers the language of fossils and dust
and once upon time there was a king et cetera
who mounted the throne to judge celestial dancers
a pair of them summoned by the vampire of the gods
so skilful with delight the ominous patter of them
resounded like lightning in a movie theater
when not even the word *silencio* brings back the dead
the prize awarded to the winner dancing bare-back
was the gift of poetry

02-20-22

VALLEJO

and my name is César, from Peru to Paris I flew my verses wild

a tropic of -isms and mineral ideologies and rainfalls

that litter the soul with caustic memories the Andes

in their entirety and doubled cathedrals mixed with sand

to weep my cause and the child lay bare to heavens

of nitrous gas and acid blares and do clouds then suffused

with sulfur and unnamed angels suffering adagios and fossils

of water the feminine in the bone the transient breath

it takes to cost a life and seasons in the mask of pain

I wear in honor of César who I am today

02-20-22

ERROR OF THE FLEETING MOMENT

two and three a fortress make of clouds

and airy azure a dream it was alive to be

some songs a darkness in the spell a dance

between breaths a comb and whispered

syllables youth a fragrance lilac or hyacinth

red ivy climbed the trellis a hand devoted

its shape to the passing breeze a ring that

cost a dime at the nickel store and books

too big to read pages too many to count

mythic afternoons spent absolutely

nowhere in the company of non-existent

nymphs whose eyes contained memory

of all the waters that have ever been and

whose hands dipped into crystal rills

streams that bore away the names we

thought were ours pronouns and masks

effigies with mortal contours and fading

into the last of the western hills a lunar

cavity with sleep the dense and eternal

could we but ever be again ! a finger

lost in grass a blade that has no edge

some words tangled up in leaves and ears

filled with archaic nonsense of poetry

standing on a distant and dusky ledge

dim figures mere shadows we discussed

the coming and going of the natural soul

the dividends of knowing when to be

and when to close the grammar of disguise

never sure which was you which was I

and leaning into the trembling light

together we paused and bade farewell

to the one and many who dwelled within

each of us the missing half of *the* other

hemispheres of unremembered dreams

lesion and clarion call the embroidery

of a single dawn so long ago so far away

whatever were we trying to say ?

whoever did we think we really were ?

02-21-22

PHILIP LAMANTIA TODAY

Philip today by no accident I stepped

on your poem engraved on Addison Street

Berkeley's subdued poetry walk in front

of a closed theater it could have been a cinema

of black swans who sing the dead forever more

or simply the crossing flash of orange death

the ritual heights of a darkened sun or asphalt

left to blare a cemetery of celestial noise

that only the archaic can hear the ones

whose literature of stone and fossil grass

whose hair and ears are known alone to bird-calls

meadowlark west ! destroyed works that

silently implore never to be published

or is it photographs passed around by fingers

of illicit descendents of bad poetic schools

crimson ledgers that   scout the air for memory

or the harassing individual who lurks in alcohol

or sells peyote buds to high school laureates ?

Philip I remember lunch with you on Columbus Avenue

your pyramid rants your mesmerized eyes

in which the Mediterranean sea turned to diamond dust

quicksilver the falsified Egypt of your mental gist

the trembling aspersions of ideologies bound

to the automatic word and least of all the possibility

of afterlife nobility among the sphinxes

who lure lanterns to their demise

Biancafiore ! your loves laid bare a hologram

of the Italian renaissance on the checkered table cloth

chianti-red and mottled like the heaven you refused

to enter on pain of losing your immortality

02-21-22

OUR CHICAGO STUDENT DAYS : THE BLUES

polyglot sky ! denatured hues of the noosphere !

immortality of ants and subsoil the Universe

mapped on the thumbnail of the corner alcoholic

and what else ? the focus of bilateral confusion

wars and intrigue lies and cheap perfumes affairs

denuded statues of Eros and the poetry of cisterns

the eluded counterpart of air transmogrified and

denied one at a time the memories of being *there*

just you and me and the blues musician's harp

the length of an afternoon in Hades subterfuge

of clouds passing through the eye of the needle

fix and fuse atomic analysis of Homeric verse

clad in mongrel outfits the Achaeans spear-first

lunging into atrocious theater-play praying loud

to the Zeus of anti-matter edges and foil argent

shining if we could wake up we would sing if we

could sing the pyramids would reverse direction

north to the southland of the living dead harmonic

convergence and riding side-saddle with Venus

into the vestibule where the *surgeon* prepares

his mnemonic device before invading the brain

is it a wonder ? grass and mouths of painted saints

opening for the ritual of the last day on earth

latitudes of fire zap ! and zing ! agonizing cries

of insects paralyzed by cosmic DDT you and me

standing there on 63rd street waiting for the jazz-club

to empty out while dawn's tequila sunrise amps

the atmosphere with literatures of surface and debate

classics ! Lucretius dangling by a hexameter an anvil

pounding BIG the mind's comedy of parallels and din

if we could wake just once again on drugged rooftops

of youth saying yes and more yes to the oncoming

galaxies of light and noise each a remembrance of when

and none the conclusion to our joy-ride to infinity

02-22-22

THE UNCOUNTED MOMENT

"la muerte es incolora, hueca, numérica", J.L. Borges

legend has it that birds and swaying things

that fly angels and learned insects weeping

in the dust of evening's fading velvet chrome

all matter of sentient beings allude to death
whose day never passes without regret and
a walking stick a path that leads to hills and
great solemn trees that converse with night
and mountaintops of nostalgia recalling
the world's empty numerical hour unseen
souls countless as sand devoured by tides
or stars that forget so often to extinguish
the birth-embers of time
explain it to me this long absence of season
of ritual of space and gravity wordless lyrics
to songs we keep on lingering light-spent
great erasures of air the ditch by the side
where the shadows went come nightfall and
when we turned to look and when the fading
in the sky was everything that wasn't meant
to be and mask and pronoun tongue and lip
stuttering aimless route to stairways leading
only half way *there* the vacant room darkening
the more as we thought to lay heavy heads
somewhere among the soiled bed-clothes
a sign the hour was up the uncounted moment
cigarette smoke thickening like omens
of distance and irreparable longing gone
all illusions the slipping away the palest ash
all burnt as the Buddha said it would be

02-23-22

ANTHROPOLOGY 101

which script we use what incisions we make

whether with a chisel or a nail-file

the result is the same bare-bones agony

dilemma of light which we can never attain

days forged in the small fires of sleep so long ago

scraping a surface looking for an entity

something that exposed to the sun will speak

get up out of bed and walk as never before

was there something before speech ?

was thought based on a pattern of signals

hands held to the air fingers alluding

to memory of eons spent in grass and rocks

listening for the sea to come rushing out of

its cave to take us by the knees and force

the issue of consciousness and identity

pronouns ! symbols for the speaker and

the spoken ruffled diagrams in the brain

pointing to the digression of hours and weeks

the simple mark on a stone regarding direction

rumors of mountains and passageways and

errors of cave and the sound of waters rolling

over adjectives and depictions on walls of

roving antlers and trees the moving spirits

that define stasis and gravity to move and be

silent in the awe of thunder and the rains and
other cloud-phenomena that herd cognition
into its compartments of noise and depths
who was the first to understand sickness ?
the entity moving between its parallel shadows
the *other* impediments of archaic emotions
the nightmare that goads battles between
families claims of land and grain and lust
spoiled dimension of barter and coinage
so much despair in the inch of centuries
thumb and index prepared to fix a target
ruminations over the wheel and how to shape it
origins of color ! pigments of blood and leaf
going in circles over the idea of time and
who can own it and how to divide it and wars !
today is no different there are beings that hide
their persons in furs and manufactured cloth
hours spent drawing maps seizing houses
inventing machines that fly imitating gods
who have perfected weapons and knowledge
information about the end of the universe !
realms of silence that have no origins
and as ever trying without succeeding
to understand *why*

02-24-22

THE POETRY LESSON

where have gone the masters of rhyme

who painted with words designs and

deceits of the gods in their cloudy mansions ?

how long without the bright of day assume

the mortal span will last and when devoured

by night will all memory disappear ?

where then are the versifiers who sought

in sounds to display the mind's unachieved

workings still-born thoughts to overcome

and disband the obstacles of dying the perfect death ?

are we speaking the same language equipped

with vowel consonant and diphthong to erect

airy chasms and celestial unrealities

prose and poetry of chimerical histories

kings and courtesans and jeweled foot-stools

ermine and plush the velvet context of error

the *pasts* ! how many of them are there

to be plundered by the hand of dreams that

yearns to rearrange falsehoods of beauty

and longing for mountains and distances

moments of an illustrated eternity childhood

brooding in twilight grasses with fingered

shadows elusive masks and pronouns

of stage-play performed in darkened mirrors

suddenly it is noon ! cognition of statues

marble come to life and jabbering in the air

birds and angels and swift intelligence of

bards and blinded serfs of knowledge

remembrances of leaf and silences of aphasia

what littered noise of cuneiform and glyph !

to write and erase and write again the idea

wheel and circumflex dialogue with the *other*

plethora of painted rock and gravel

homecomings and love in the dripping eaves

a lifetime is short and bitter the fading

purple of a sunset off Hesperian shores

or the cliff where unidentified persons

who strangely resemble *you and me*

park their metal chariot to stare

characters of disposable unities and bliss

discharge of echoes ! to hear just once the poem

then to sleep the infinite inch of night

02-25-22

ON THE PUBLICATION OF MY MILLIONTH BOOK !

to wake up on the night that follows infinity

what does the number five matter ?

repercussions of the last known asterisk in space

Miles Davis wearing a zoot-suit stolen from Lorenzo de' Medici

playing music from the Roman Empire loud and with grief

standing there a-glitter the pomp of his hair !

to read and read again the license to employ the same vowel

over and over and the burden of the years that supersede

the several inches of mown grass or the futile spark

lit by the first gram of alcohol to ignite the blood

I am nothing if not the remaining half of a conjunct consonant

the sometimes unfit syllable in phonetic decay

a linguistic disorientation x-rayed and pre-conditioned

for a width of bad poetry diagnosis ranting off color

who was that girl-goddess anyway ? why did it take so long ?

avenues that yawn out into the brief eternity of high school

nexus and preponderance of red-litmus the poetry

of make-believe behind sand bags and crumbling stucco walls

this is not the second or third time but not the final either

when the Mayo Clinic takes center place in my biography

a curbstone and filtered cherry cokes and blackened mirrors

a glass of refined ethyl in front of the court house

vocalic dysentery using only Mexican digraphs imagining

the highway that *only* goes east to destroyed cities

to places evacuated by the *arhats* driving diesel fuel trucks

jukebox memory of the time we climbed the pyramids

down in dusky Teotihuacan when the sun stood still

just long enough for the photographs to develop

showing twins transmogrified by an unidentified flying object

a scanning device that only recognizes hieroglyphs

it keeps on happening the inner echo of the Muse

whose voice was turned off centuries ago in a maelstrom

caused by the unexpected and epic conclusion to a planet

whose noontime was a devotional of statuary and caryatids

massive sleep inhibition talking backwards to a reflection

traveling at light years per second and I am still here !

02-26-22

THE PENULTIMATE DAY OF BREATH

whose was the radiant body ?
who was the fish caught in the red doorway ?
whose was the shadow that would not be released ?
whose were the hands that turned to burning cellophane ?
who came in second without distinction ?
whose was the bitumen and the aggravation ?
loaded into the back seat of the car half-conscious
who was the adolescent without memory ?
whose were the meadows and corn-fields of cognition ?
who was the outline with antlers at the window ?
how did this come to be stagecraft or monopoly ?
religion ! the twenty feet between here and the next life !
messages arrive daily written on scraps of paper

or the backs of discarded envelopes bills and subterfuge

who was he anyway ? stuttering and stammering

a grammar in disguise a polyvalent consonant

a mesmerized attitude about love some vowels

scattered across the patchwork quilt of hills

that dominate the western view from the balcony

whose is the finger lost forever in the darkness of grass ?

a bell ! determination to give up thinking

to audit the chaos that dwells in the basement

to slam the door shut on memories and x-rays

who was admitted to heaven without shoulders ?

grief ! the fifty-five platitudes about sorrow

the weeping in the corridors waiting for an automobile

horses of the sun ! motionless muscles and fly-swarms

perspiration of the gods ! immense distances of water

fanning out over the nearest galaxy

positions of latent philosophy ! one two but never three

edges of words that define the sound of sleep

the minute orchestras of moths and lightning-bugs

interred in the ear at the bottom of stone

whose is the poem about celestial corpses ?

I am ! there is a moment of infinite silence

who is the girl third from left in the daguerreotype ?

are there only nine mazes in the portfolio ?

are footsteps articulate ? is there a   flower-bed to step on ?

so much nuisance and noise all in dialect !

tomorrow will be different !

02-27-28

NUMEROLOGY

the enormous lies of literature !

Hector or Achilles assured the futility of immortal fame

and Dionysus or Apollo divinities of booze and mice

to what avail prayers to their blowzy essences ?

at the feet of Minerva fall and ask for redemption

if not life everlasting and knowledge that survives death

each number becomes more difficult to pronounce

the world is nothing if not error and rumor

medical advice bad prescriptions faulty x-rays

in jeopardy the total hemisphere of innocence

the unsuspecting child with a cold sore in his mouth

the ambulance out of control crossing invisible bridges

mythology of the numbers four or forty

superseding vowels and cataracts of words without edges

slide-shows depicting the end of civilization by social-media

thumb-nail portraits in ancient cuneiform

revealing monarchs the size of bees or wasps

the Hummingbird triumphant on the pyramid of the Sun

plastic play-toys designed to fly like UFOs

across the backyard where shadows of grass call out

for the kids who used to leap and spear their *others*

and totem beasts who govern hospitals and research

and declare the finitude of all disease in literary format

nothing ! death still seizes us by the knees from behind

rooms open and close upon formal religions

leaving all speculation to shaman and haruspex

steaming innards of holy deer and noon time heat

sun in its eternal elasticity roaring like wounded rock

in the eclipse of a page of history and nothing !

grief is the surfeit the envelope of shorn hair

the adolescence never attained the summer-long coma

the unpunctuated universe of haunting silence

hands that reach for memory of shape and distance

how many mountains have intervened since then ?

we go back to the infantile solemnities

to visions of snow greater than its hidden metals

to streets of late Italian prosody charged with infinity

nothing lasts ! obdurate masks that govern mirrors

and the deceived who are left to sorrow in a garden

littered with the broken hieroglyphs of ants

the enormous lies of literature !

Diana has spent her shafts in the unbidden heart

four years now that are no more than four minutes

in the expanding number which is death

Max obit Feb 28, 2018

02-28-22

THE SECOND DAY OF DEATH

and on the second day was the silence any greater ?
did murmurs from the other side seem more indistinct ?
whose was the shadow whitening slowly on the stucco wall ?
picking overripe plums from the corner of the lawn
that's what was left of memory a siege of innuendos
turning west toward the oblique light of the former sun
legends and half-truths the vestige of cognition fading
words eaten by the moths of oblivion sounds and hues
everything retreating into a lapse of phonetics and tone
hands suffering loss of shape ears at one with stone
echoes of stars that died three million light years ago
the slightest vowel the pinch of green that lingers
over grass mown seasons ago and crickets and fireflies
cornfields lush with heat blackening in the afternoon's
brief eternity so much and so many things that no longer
fit description just the small ricochet and rattle of toys
in a department store basement or the reading of consonants
in the ritual that closes parks at sundown and the chill
the ensuing threat of frost and decimation of numbers
nothing more to contain in the zero that precedes
the end of time the transmogrification of marble into
ciphers senseless matter the opalescent moon standing
upright for a few more minutes before turning ruddy then
pale yellow merging with the vertigo of bees when winter

arrives with its sheets and skirts of total darkness

night dreamless and limited to a few strokes of the brush

inky clouds billowing from the far origins of space

and the body inert mass of cooling temperatures that

lies in wait for the love that transcends understanding

03-01-22

THE GREAT GATE OF KIEV

the great antiquities have come and gone !

honey-bees courtesans mango blossoms confused

as to which dialect to use to express great suffering

entrances and exits of buffoons and gamblers the grief !

absence of snow and burning cornfields distances

too narrow to observe and the mountain talking

in its sleep oracular and infantile hoarse cataracts

poverty ! decimation of logic cognition and reason

the king needs his opium ! sewers running with gold

attendants and slaves waking to another day of doubt

which is the stairway that goes up ? freedom from remorse !

which are the animals and which the refugees of war ?

the people are in need of paper and instructions

none of the philosophers have left the cave

warning signals in the shape of asterisks and commas

mark the air with coruscations and fireflies

orthographies of incomprehensible beauty and disaster

how many times was the reading interrupted ?

the great antiquities have come and gone !

rubble and transport of consonants and rhetoric

ruins of language deficit of vowels shortage of marble

analphabetic statues in need of humanitarian aid

whole continents submerged overnight ! Byzantium !

what is memory of red silk and oiled skins baths

and the tumult of salts and license to pray ?

the sun is only half its light and its steeds collapsed

and the hour has just begun ! cities that transgress

gardens and moons and priests running amok

in the holy groves where spotted deer nibble on sound

the famous rivers have lost their way ! drought

famine missing shorelines and total phonetic decay

inarticulate planets out of alignment at high noon !

hospitals and opprobrium faulty medicine transplants

overdose and dementia ! what's left of the Book ?

the great antiquities have come and gone !

03-02-22

THE TWINS NEITHER HERE NOR THERE

bewildering as ever the possibilities of what might

have been *if* and always the conditional that stuns

bees in their midday riot or turns snow to metal

who was the stranger that give us the one-way ticket

sleep folded over and over to wake on the other side

of a poem which has no beginning yet finds us lost

in the tempestuous middle with neither side visible

a baffle of identities learning to drive or attempt suicide

with glass broken in violent contours and blood fresh

as the spring day we learned there was no other way

out of the maze but to climb and descend the same stairs

in a repetition of memories and smoking one more

marijuana cigarette and making faces in the mirror

as if to exchange the future for an unknown immortal past

what days ! rivers and willow trees and endless grass

how did we become uprooted from our brief paradise

to weathers and time-zones hostile to our green budding

was anything ever really the way it turned out to be ?

drugs splicing atmospheres that smothered the light

advancing ever southwards to the base of the pyramid

of eternal noon ! music and fossil candidates for

a degree in art history and theories and conjectures

ranging from the wildest Homeric theogony to

the surrealist who invented the negative personality

we were there fitting one suit after another getting

ready to dance with Fata Morgana or Persephone

deaths by the number reverberating in the alcohol

and tobacco that converted us into reflections imitating

cinematic ephemeral gods and what else but the Wheel

and the indentation in space and suns of glittering tinsel

the eye rapt with dimensions of other universes

those of the *tlaloc* and *mechica* tribes blazing

with the adolescent infinities we assumed were ours

you and me Bro' speculative idiomatic speech acts

jabbering backwards in the hiatus between the night

of the womb and the numerical hallucination of time

03-04-22

I READ THE NEWS TODAY OH BOY !

great the numinous and unrecorded deeds of the ancients !

speculative imitation of sleep boundless and unique

embroidering texts of glyph and rumor in decibels

too high to resonate in the passionate ear of leaf and stone

who was the first ? what was the commemoration of fire ?

when going round and round with a single sound mortals

tried to bring the deity to light with shape and memory

to no avail ! eons of a-historical events weaponry and gadgets

of paint and smoke the thunder of theaters copies

of waters tumultuous and rare with salt-sprays that

touch the heavens and brooding figures lamenting losses

the longing that surpasses life and enormous statues of air
listing breaking apart over the waves and technologies
of the aleph and supreme entelechy walking the shores
early dawn of the mind ! a wonder to read in a blade of grass
the future of the universe symbols and aggregations of noise
the births and only death ! how did we come to dwell in this ruin ?
summations of the number three in its boomerang and dialect
foment and parody of adulthood spackled against a mirror
of painted glass the dark movements of human animals
descending from the hill into the valley of remorse
deafening silence of iniquities and justifications of cash
and capital and torment dividing the self from its *other*
cities like bombs ! hands that mark the end of the hour
with immense red symbols and diacritics and words
unspoken never illustrated meaningless entombed
in the variable lexicon of error and thought
have we come to announcing wars as if they were toys !
tanks versus girls on streets turned to rubble the opaque
language of the video-gram the platforms of mendacity
superfluous commodities x-rays of the nuclear eclipse
a thousand and eight suns immolated on the Eiffel Tower !
it goes on and on the fuming and famous *et cetera*
divinations and lightning-rods the tiny radios of aphasia
there is no definition of breath that doesn't' contain death
we move secretly from sleep to sleep becoming ghosts
samples of artificial intelligence repercussion of vowels
aimed at the moon's invisible bedlam a mountain tossed

on its side beside the astronomy of preterit mythologies

we are nothing if not vague ! wrecks and shadows outlines

on burning concrete the nightmare of small consonants

issuing like news out of the oracle of mismanagement

and space the entirety of its uncontainable inch !

which one are you ? the haunted house

03-04-22

THE GRAMMAR OF MIRRORS

everything is a copy of everything else

the inverse is the reverse and yet nothing

resembles the imitation of this copy unless it is

the infinite extent of the daily azure

fingering remoteness of cloud and unseen anchor

seas of billowing eternity the size of sleep

and to look again and echo with one's own form

the rectitude of memory into eyes collapsed

by darkness and nothing is a centimeter off

precisely and exactly as one appears so one is

vanishing in the ready-made function of reflections

imitations of marble echoes of rock and cliff

grassy inundations of time in a speculative drift

from the only possible hour when the senses

collapse in sheets of undulating waters

reveries of a past without repercussion resonance

and abatement of consciousness the perfect
amalgam of tense and chronology fiction
and error of time-keeping illustrated matter
turning the pages of an imaginary reader
of all ancient languages staring deep into the void
where words decay and the phonology of cognition
bright for just a moment evaporates and the harsh
sun of unreason with its revolving homophones
struggles to hold noon back from its wild horses
and yet here you stand hemispheres of irreconcilable
illusions putting one hand to the left which becomes
the hand on the right a judgment of aphasia and silence
the witless discrepancies of vision and rumor
the fluidities of persona and mask fugue and
discipline of noise the wave-length of distance
mountains that intercede between dreams
of the self becoming the *other* always coming back
to that isolation of space-and-time the mirror
irrevocable glass suspended from the laws
of ether and dynamics the refutation
of the *known* even as you keep gazing
into the crypt of your own being the thing
you can never really know as illusory as *light*
that both determines and dissolves shapes
yourself infinite and deluded repetition
of *yourself yourself yourself*

03-05-22

ROUNDELAY

five in the afternoon again !

how can that be ? it was only yesterday this morning

and tomorrow with fragrances of death and roses

has already come and gone ! agonies of counting

backwards into the sleep of margins

or to host the decayed vowel in its teacup of solemnities

a guitar on the wall the singing fabric of lunacy

why we do consecrate each minute with a separate

memory when all ages are one and silences reign

in the cosmic design of annulled personality ?

what's the temperature today ? how many times will it rain ?

so long ago it was and not too far away we lived a dream

mountains and dense woods the poetry of make-believe

we worked and played and danced a night or two

the song was tremulous the voices a bric-a-brac of sound

distances ! we varied the hour of day and settled plans

to never move again to remember that lingering

and longing were what remained and each calendar

was a thing to destroy and how we loved in the vacuum

of the weeks that passed in mourning grief and sorrow

what's on the schedule for this evening ? the roles of fief

and kingship the suits of armor the clay idols

stirring in their niche of borrowed light the Spanish lesson

with its play of honorific pronouns the disguise of ladders

and broken necks the insufferable lament in Andaluz

it all comes back the round of strife and depth

the skies that open wide their small eternities

to let enter the least of our bereaved angels

step by step the smoke of lies disintegrates

life finds us soon on the other side of time

diction and euphoria madness and repercussion

five in the afternoon again !

03-06-22

THE WEEK THAT NEVER WAS

seas of cognition fill the ear's secret drum

and fading evidence of light on earth

buried in urns made by ancient gods

rows of signs immortal glyphs

fingers of lithe grass at twilight legends

writ of soil and catastrophe a human thought

undone by medication and a fatal vowel

the lingering of the archaic soul in its husk

skin and tissue elements of lasting doubt

the world's smallest member without a voice

machines pumping imitations of breath

what is no more the number of days

that comprise a simple week

names ! echoes of leaf and gravel

verbiage of wind in the solemn hill

where shadows play with dark silhouettes

to succumb in the silent roaring of a star

lifted from its ossuary and made to shine

to mask despair with gravity and speed

outlast distance ! fix the moving dart

in its choir of multiple directions and

no more grieve the emptied noun

counting each faint sound a whisper

that lasts more than one eternity

remembering that what the fever hid

was the child infinitely ten

Max

03-07-22

ORPHEUS TODAY

I am considering a book

called Craving Death

not the literal kind that rushes

the seashores with broken knees

nor the salt-spume that sprays

the mind's orphic eye of despair

but the red light of the other world

the symptom of gravity and loss

that burdens too many a mortal shoulder

and to behold in the looking-glass

that silhouette of darkening trust

Eurydice on her backward path to hell

such a yearning I cannot dispel

so much longing to mate with death

the passions of light and fantasy

are but detritus of the errant brain

a sophist leaning toward definition

when nothing can be defined if not

the great unknown the misspent idylls

of prolonged youth the arcadian cliff

from which we all must jump

yes I crave all deaths to make

my one death the easier to bear

03-07-22

TESTIMONIAL

I have been witness to the world

have seen its rarities and encumbrances

wrath and total denial its box of history

stolen jewels and laments the crucifix

in the desert the rats and elephants and

hills teeming with dialects and swarms
of insects in clouds traveling across sutures
wounded and divided the plots of land
the scoured waters with no depths shallows
the narrow sequence between then and now
whispers and antinomies and strutting like
parades of color the masks of letters and
silt and rutting numbers the breadth
and longitude of continents swamped by
details of heat no longer assuaged by lies
about temperature and its range of motion
or was it merely the stalled memory of defiles
invasions of language in the bottom-lands
conquests by gravity of lunar distances
and the months of aggravation and armies
on stilts and circus make-up trapeze and rope
climbing the mountain's missing side a last
and longing breath in crowded hospital wards
the child and his hands confused as to direction
south is up north is gone nowhere in sight
the juntas and reprisals of myth and idiom
subtexts and corollaries resonating in seas
that have been bought and sold too many times
antiquities that persist in illegible accounts
of the sack of Troy metaphors and diatribe
literatures of assonance and retribution
each has as many dreams as sleep's surfeit

of forgotten verse legendary and haunting

echo of Cassandra's voice on the stairs

a cigarette a void a love-letter misplaced

spatial punctuations and perforated metal

junk accumulating where oceans used to be

panoply of sounds emitted by radios loud

useless pronouncements about death and wires

transfusions and pyramids radiating music

how many times did I witness the ascent

of ghosts splintered consonants the effort

to piece together a speech act and logic

woeful the assemblage of leaves weeping

in the dark and grasses torn harrowing

repetitions of air an unknown goddess

mysterious and sibylline whose vanishing

is the question mark of immortality

03-08-22

FACING EAST

Max on his 54th birthday

seeing you as you walked the pre-dawn streets

accompanied by white-robed priests of Horus

ha pepi pu !

vision of the star still buried in the eastern Mound

how magnificent you were all height and stride
ready to greet and bless the impoverished homeless
                      and unaware
the *Fish* in the sky ! radiant freed from
the tumultuous liquid straits of time *shone*
invisible to all but you intent on your passage
from the earth of x-rays and futile transfusions
the disciples of rain were preparing their dialect
unbeknownst to us incapable of fathoming distances
greater than the few inches that separate the muezzin's
first cry of the day from the sun's black homophone
what was the human voice ? in your ear the satellites
of memory and grass were set on the great dissolution
distinctions of hour and hue of ant and bee of footfalls
like the arguments of medical savants nothing but detritus
the worlds of pre-birth the immense incongruities
of gravity and space travel and illumination from within
shopping basement stores Saturday mornings !
sidewalks rippling with continents of play and noise
always the hand extended to embrace the fallen !
one two and then three the boomerang of Love !
we held you one last time though you never knew it
the disciples of rain ! headlights of the gods nine days
from infinity making way for the seraphic wing
ascent and disappearance drizzle of ash and light
the harp's plangent notes the burning garlands
somewhere in the maze of truths and hypocrisies

you remained the evidence of determination and grit

spectral and luminous in today's darker heavens

your spirit flitting among the unheard notes of planets

that arrived too late for the noon of your departure

facing east in search of the bridge of Mysteries

                    for Marilla and Alexander

03-09-22

ELEGY : MARCH 9, 2022

is there some way to reconstruct the immemorial

moments which today are only havoc of noise and error ?

the functions of grass the evenings of leaves

longing to overcome night's extended infinity of asterisks

we ask but never stay long enough for the answer

uncontained and void our beings go wandering

lost in the multiple number that precedes zero and

whatever can be said there are no imitations of life

no breath that goes on forever past the stone lying

in the field that marks the division between light

and the underground where Persephone at play with

tiny houses and the images of death does not cease

weeping at recordings of her summer days in time

such as we are flitting vagabonds of shadow poems

inextricable sounds in the laboratory of metaphors

hands that ply the looms of distance anatomy and specter

fusion of scripts and dichotomies of meaning

for which of us is meant the plagiarized event and

for whom the inconsequential oblivion of this day ?

03-09-22

THE HIGH-SCHOOL BAEDEKER

we have passed through the lands of lateral ecstasies

and traded camels for mountains in the defiles

we have been devoured by the natural language of birds

and copulated with insensate deities traversing

distances the size of thumb-nails or shop-windows

we have accomplished poetry and illusion metaphor

and the subjunctive clauses of denial and repercussion

enormous have been our tragedies assimilations of death

and the tremendous waters beneath all depths of sound

nothing and to no avail our transcendences of empire

our glottal stops our diphthongs and mesmerizing dots

whatever we have achieved is not ours to claim

like the goddess we cannot possess the worlds of thought

the least and most diminutive of scales the echelons

of mounting cipher and hue none of that is ours

schisms of memory and rock formations immense

speculations of the extent of night in the spatial dome

regrets and remorse that we ever loved without gravity

we presume to have arrived but where ? asterisk

of incognito and surrealism our beings hesitate

decorating mirrors with watch-fobs and iotas

intellect has never been our strength nor the will

to determine and longing for otherness we gather

unknown any more to one another beneath the Hill

demesnes and potters' fields grammar of the unseen

listening to voices torn from leaves and Homeric echolalia

we remain confused masks and pronouns forged entities

in the legendary fix of nomenclature and schizophrenia

what are we but copies of thread-bare planets

caroming in misinformed halls of the Zodiac

it is high noon ! blood surfaces like steam on metal

surfaces the projected empyrean of gas and alcohol

multiplied by zero ! we map history with small letters

in cuneiform or waxen glyphs and pray to mythic gods

rulers of pyramid and song sorrowing the withered plant

aggrieved at all the children lost senseless and beautiful

on the enigmatic and circular route of infinity

03-10-22

CHANSON DE GESTE

para mi hermana

remember when we played dead in the back yard ?
the world was a secret only we knew and nobody else
who was that desperado cowboy who killed us riding a horse
stolen from Saturday afternoon movies in black and white noise ?
thunder and explosions of light resounded in our ears
and the grass bent down to listen as we became shadows
instantaneous copies of ourselves refulgent and unconscious
how many years passed in that instant of dying so quickly
eternities of sun-blots and a desert of nightly asterisks
laughing at our secret ambitions we traded silks and
sombreros and clambered aboard the empty stage-coach
waiting for Lash Larue to whip up a storm between meals
the willow tree was the soul of the afternoon plaintive
with its forty thousand leaves all speaking Mexican and
if others came to look what did they find but our blood
leaking invisible as gasoline all over the canyon's depths
how far away the moon was at three PM all lusterless
a cavern of distance lacking memory and us in a lather
to get back on our mounts firing our cap pistols in the air
who were those young poets who never went to war ?
a screen door opened and slammed shut or was it
the hound of hell that woke us momentarily in a bar
where artists in black neckties and drinking sarsaparilla
paused to aim their bottles at us lying there in sawdust
suddenly we got up brushing the summer weeds off us

capsized from one life into another we cavorted happy

that we could finally go home freed from the calaboose

of infinite time and heat and the dizzy spectacle of kids

all come back to life running across the street to

houses dark and vacant as abandoned ice-boxes

---

the radio shows that night were full of masked villains

mysterious pilots of unidentified flying objects that hovered

above earth waiting to snatch the souls of twins and the like

and hide them beneath the great pyramids forever

AOI

03-11--22

HOMAGE TO JORGE LUIS BORGES

verisimilitude of the poem in question

metaphors of age and height and longing

caught in mid-flight air no longer matters

of no consequence breath to recite immortal

verses the similes and hash-tags and sorrow

what doesn't last what little counts the siege

of language and its thousand splintered ideolects

woods and rosaries inaugural events in chiaroscuro

boulevards equal in length to eternity's half mile

visions ! cauterized wounds of triremes tarred

and fissured the atomic valence of sound and
whatever else matches memory in durability
among the pointillistic heavens of sleep
the empty name the possession of reality
the multiple stairways with as many cigarettes
twice the number of photographs in one dream
about double armies exercising the right to bridge
remnants of space its hills and folded grasses
hospitals on terraced slopes smoke signals
the wanderers who have come to a standstill
where the roads separate and a voice takes over
loud and gravid the distinctions disappear and
bereft of virtues day-stars come crashing
through awnings and shops filled with tourists
repetitions of the poem ! the many and the untold
evacuation of the senses illusory courtyards
one leading to another bejeweled caparisoned
with horses drawn from still-life and arches
and domes and vestibules and imaginary
as always princesses hoodwinked by fate
to remain poor and unendowed but for a secret
to remain a secret forever ! which is the poem
and who is the reader and how many lines
have been erased to be re-created in another life
I was there first ! a Morris dance on the lawn
mounds of dialects heretical symbols glyphs

and graphs where words argue with *words*
about the place of noise in the rhyme scheme
and the poem as ever puzzling digamma and
bolt of aspersions love and its tonics springtime
the birth of Venus ! too many books and
antiquities of meaning enigmas without variation
endless philosophies about the letter *"H"*
augurs dressed in zoot suits clambering for
a meal and entrails left steaming an alphabet
celestial and dubious and no one is allowed
entrance to the place where enshrined by critics
the poem dissolves illegible faintly beautiful
the pallid representation of a life however brief
that cannot be reconciled with its artistic depiction
gods and mummers ! waxen images of the sun !
from afar the poets have come with their mountains
their small grasp of the seas their blindness and
lack of memory and composing in a trance
the verbiage and nonsense of literature
awards and cinema of death

03-12-22

THE TRANSFORMATIONS OF LANGUAGE

the insignificant paralysis of the sky *today*
resorting to a past as irretrievable as it is indistinct
amalgam of noise and silence clouds erupting
though magnums of orange and violent flashes
meaningless symposium of azure and distance
untranslatable as each eon becomes a dialect
and each dialect a wound in the invisible body
what are the attributes of sound ? where are they ?
we wander raveling texts of sleep and dominion
and nothing really wakes plant or demon hesitant
in the wings of a mansion dedicated to gods
who are waiting to be born aching in the dream
of being and becoming and whenever the ear stirs
reacting to patterns of tone and accent and seas
come rushing like half-empty vessels of light
towards the mountain where language incubates
we persist in taking pronouns and masks and hail
the latest innovation in speech as a law and
regard with awe the transformations of syntax
words tumble forth like fogs in the spare light
of this diminished day and routines of graph
and glyph and chiseled metrics in stone and
reductions of the absurd to quantum mechanics
so many exercises to escape the thought of dying
somnolence and vagrancy through parks and
woods labyrinthine as poetry in its origins

trying and failing trying and failing to utter
correctly the formulae of transcendence and
salvation and like myrmidons plaguing the shores
with our tents and camp-fires praying for the dawn
was there ever greater license to abound and kill ?
everywhere it says ditto and reprise and recommence
the graduates of last year are dead ! whole sections
of atmosphere and memory excised irrevocable
and fleeting the tender moments of love and grief
when were we ever able to express with feeling ?
rumor and error of warfare and plights booming
in the shelled citadel of longing and fingers running
over verses of grass and leaf and the evidence of
history nothing but clods of dirt ant-mounds small
lesions in the revolving earth of piety and gnosis
today as never before the yawning abyss unreason
misuse of logic reiterations of escape clauses
folly of semantics and desecrations of the heart
ambulances veering out of control in the galaxies
punctuations intended to ease understanding
lost in the menacing flux of cosmic data and !
talk of the angels and the final subtleties
beyond human ken

03-13-22

A FINAL CONVERSATION

and the gods assembled from the ten universes
for what reason ? as examples of grammar
paradigms and injunctions singular and plural
manifestations of water and its absence the whole
without its parts infinitives and absolutives
stopping to pause between cosmic breaths and
radiant as only deities can be in the instant of
automatic self-incineration and what else matters
in the totality of sound and nothingness ? silence
the intaglio of fire the brimming bottle of mystery
one and two and three the thing that can never
come back on its own standing on the dance of time
the appearance of mirrors without reflections
the parsed sentence of poetry the inevitability
of death and rain and of the nine remaining
universes which is the puzzle which is the answer
margins and bottomless seas and shorelines fade
and the perpetuity of sleep after life the simple
fix of breath and illusion heat going in circles
divisions of number into ever more infinite units
and phonetic decay the largesse of immobility
assumptions about magnetism and the compass
polar densities frozen copulas between sessions
how else can the deities gain on their unknown past ?

and thirty-one eons from now when the mind

is freed from influxes neither looking up

nor looking back when all has come to naught and

from all perceived directions the self-same flame

goes out and the body obtains its seventh heaven

the great inertia of oblivion and fame then what voice

or what verb tense and dislocation will prevail ?

the incomplete illusion the half-frozen photograph

capturing the soul's moment of departure from thought

conversation between the parallel selves the halves

with nowhere to turn but the ancient and innocent

extension of speech into myth embroidered consonants

notched on antler bone of the roving beast whose

night is a cave of attitudes and fears the lessening

day the former nights centuries of upheaval between

brother and brother a hand brought forward to mouth

the final words whispers conjectured synthesis of

noise before the spool unwinds and a symphonic version

of the color red in its mortal hiatus so Greek in value

and rendered nil after four decades of struggling

to keep it animate and meaningful to what avail ?

we talk back and forth between the sheets yellow

with fever and ague the ages of archaic language

resolutions and divisiveness of maps left in the rain

obliterating the possibilities of homecoming to what ?

darkened houses lawns in quiet upheaval History !

yet we keep talking despite the telephone and its
limited combination of numbers and the hour's up
and the sashes have been drawn and the weary
enfeebled portfolio of flowers fading like twilight
among the rock formations the trilobite embedded
in its vowel the importunate song of the dead moon
passed through the clepsydra and symbol of space
what can we never finish saying ? amen and amen
the peace that passes understanding

03-14-22

CONFESSIONS OF AN ANONYMOUS POET

sunshine arrives late on the patio of planet Yucatan
revolving in a mimicry of galaxies in a sovereign
space no greater than the diameter of a speculative eye
sporting the pool of desires and refrain and splash !
incongruous fictions methodologies of fantasy
the resonance of an ear in phonetic decay asleep
driving the engine of noises far from its origins
a poetry and incunabula of narrative gist
high romance in the Pyrenees and with Oliver
and Roland in complete despair how does the author
retrieve the horn ? atrocities of the pronoun !

unpredicted weathers in a gorgeous plumage

of adjectives functioning as truths and offenses

the choice to make among so many deaths

and the equilibrium of light expanding as it does

unconsciously and into directions too remote

for argument like sleep like grass like stone that

borders margins of the childhood path to hell

this is either the first or the last of poetries assonance

of gold and flawed silver assemblies that by noon

are rocked by havoc and scandal monarchic as

the bedlam that belittles the excess of desire

yes that and more followed by exclamation marks !!!

and the entire tale of Sinbad adventures in music

and telephones and bric-a-brac of long distance calls

to the unknown dead buried in the heart's graveyard

I am other than Orestes ! I am warfare and the plague

of modernity and post-secularism and the rights

for centrifuge fuels and license to betray earth

fuming roundelays of memory and idiomatic voices

Electra ! falsified documents of love and tempests

the thin membrane between reason and madness

Mexican dialects of blood and smoking hands that

burn to contain the sun's vast error through time

poverty and nonchalance of the Universe ! *italics*

and bedrock the thought that abandons the soul

in the end like Iphigenia ! let the fleets go disordered

ready to turn to flame and holocaust of Troy

whiplash lingerie of Aphrodite ! there is *no one*

writing these automatic absences of word and

subterfuge collected dots ampersands and asterisks

the heavens afloat with nemesis and retribution !

and made to talk as if the *other* and to sing !

03-15-22

MY FATHER'S GREEN CARD

  para mi querida hermana Laurita

the Eisenhower fifties
 Don't let the stars get in your eyes
driving his second-hand chevy into the hoosegow
 Don't let the moon break your heart
careful not to let go of his green card
Enrique Argüelles takes a break from mural-painting
snoozes down in the basement with copies of Esquire
and dreams of Jalisco and mountains like burnt thimbles
problems of English phonetics and German in-laws
forced to go to church violating his rights
freedom to choose antipathies and –isms
pounding his chest saying proudly *Soy Comunista* !
somewhere in the newsreels Popocatépetl is smoking
a pack of Pall Mall cigarettes a day and doesn't fear

Joe McCarthy or the local Kiwanis club and sneers
contemptuously at the farmers who bring their goods
Saturdays crowding South Broadway with their trucks
knowing his Aztec intelligence is far superior
careful not to let his green card go astray
even as he wastes hours in Darst's Bar & Grill
nursing one Pabst Blue Ribbon after another and
eyeing the calendar girl pinned to the wall
in her scanty blonde see-through polka dot blouse
a pair of grease-monkeys named Bud and Eddie egg him on
laughing at his bad command of American peppered
with Mexican idiolect all *carajo* and *chingada*
the plate glass window with its flushed red neon
reflects his profile handsome cinematic Latin Lover
with Clark Gable moustache and bedroom eyes
his head ricochets with songs by Trio Los Panchos
as he makes his way to the garage with Bud and Eddie
where they fool around polishing off another six-pack
before he gets back into the chevy imagining
he is driving down Avenida Insurgentes and not
First Avenue SW pressing the accelerator a bit too hard
is it night or day ?

  Las veces que me ha visto llorar

   La perfidia de tu amor

everything is doused in atmosphere of Lutheran church
wooden pews and stern sermons about death and hell
yellow pink and blue tulips do not diminish it

Sundays are an infernal version of eternity

exiled roaming the sullen neighborhoods like

a billiard ball caroming on the green baize surface

of unrelenting penance alcohol and more alcohol

arriving home three AM with San Juan de la Cruz who

carries his piano into a corner of the living room

his hands alternate *Für Elise* with *Bésame mucho*

making sure the green card was still in his pocket

as his head magnificent with wavy black hair perfectly

undulated and in place nods off into Lomas Chapultepec

and the Toltec sun burning riotously black and pure

in the language of Cuauhtémoc and Lázaro Cárdenas

lost in the cruel dream-spell of History with his every move

carefully scrutinized by the Mayo Clinic

> *Las veces que me ha visto llorar*
>
> *La perfidia de tu amor*

denizen of Sears and Roebuck basement sales

wearing cast-off suits and painting painting painting

to get back something of the solar destiny he left behind

in the pyramids his twis sons had conquered

one inevitable and infinite summer day of 1953

and always soiled and dog-eared stashed in his wallet

the green card which by old age was totally useless

a citizen of nowhere painting painting painting

> *To you my heart cries out "Perfidia"*

03-15-22

UNKNOWING

for Solomon Rino

life is unbearably sweet and poignant today

why go on living ? does rain wear its cathedrals

of unseen light for a reason ? why are the doves

white and intransigent cooing in the eaves of doubt ?

the ceramics of grief painted with double stripes

of vermillion and mystery are set upon the table

for all to behold and yet and yet the windows weep !

how ancient it all is as if duplication of memory

were not sufficient and the double-bass of threnody

runs its counterpoint through our waking sleep

why does it have to be just one way and not the other ?

look ! the sky is a small pool waiting for its cloud

to reverse direction and this summer is all summers

past unnamable and without punctuation and is it

a wonder the sarcophagus has no children ? fret

and strife the echolalia of the earthly passage

we go tuning the instrument listening intently for

thunder to break open its theater of tragedies

it is just so today the intensity of feeling in one finger

while the rest of the hand goes numb in the weeds

looking for the *Vita Nuova* despite the darkening

delved into the wood the verses and incantations

of the unheard voice mourning its lost signals

yes and for once the dialect and its phonetic other

have taken the hill of objections and the funeral
of light ! wearing suits of solar blackness we sit dumb
on the ridge of time watching cranes and swans
form alphabets in the nuance of the heavens a sight
to behold this joy and shivering ! muses beware !
this *book* has no readers ! what day is yesterday ?
is it the same as every day at four in the afternoon
when the pilgrims arrive in their shiny new sedans ?
the plenitude that fills the heart is it because
this day withdraws its name ? unknowing !

03-16-22

PHANTOM TRAVELERS

"Todo acontece y nada se recuerda",

J.L. Borges,

a valley without a shadow an ego without a pronoun
wherever we go walking in this confused chiaroscuro world
what's the difference between life and death
a mirror of speculation endless and undetermined
phantoms and imitations crying for their past
unredeemable moments spent thoughtlessly
on love or gain and to turn the corner and find
the mask is not there the person long abandoned
by the body and the heights and corollaries of cloud

and red lightning musk and lotus stalk the whole panoply
of image and technique a fool's game of illusion and
literature the mountain that intervenes between
consciousness and the black realms that lie beyond sleep
inability to count past three before falling forever
looking around with hands that gesture for the light
to reappear and for language to assume some role
in the daily casualty lists and encounters with ghosts
why am I here at all ? the resident alien in the house
next door looks just like us ! nevertheless the symptoms
of make-believe and synchronicity prevail with all
their diacritics and nuances and we take for granted
that the following day really is possible that once
we anchor the reflection to its glass gravity will cease
to matter and though our accomplishments remain
they are but memories fogs and perishable stone ink
and sand and shorelines that come running breathlessly
to take us by the knees and bring on the night
how do we get past the coming traffic signal ?
to go to bed with maximum confusion as to who it is that
is falling asleep inside our head ! travelers we wake
in a nameless motel on an unmarked route and longing
and grief wherever we look in this persistent vertigo
we mistake for life

                (para Armando Rendón)

03-17-22

ELEGY : MARY LOU FOREVER

unheeded the signal that identifies eternity

repetition of a lyric in a dance song darkened

October nights swelling distance dimly glowing

hand-held bouquets and pronouns exchanged like flames

too late the screen to keep the fireflies out their number

an increase in the dominion of the *unknown* flitting

flickers once then goes out like breath the life-source

vague rumors that everything really will end and none

will be the wiser for the mistaken steps or the blown

hilarity of a myth charades of adolescence and youth

sound of metal and speed and drams of consciousness

distributed unevenly among the cherished few

faces that become indistinct error and metaphor

let alone the names which are as leaves falling in

the autumn whirl maze and hues of infinite regret

who will ever remember with clarity the introduction ?

by accident the planets come into view and hover

into an opaque nomenclature of scientific speculation

not like the persons they represent flashing on and off

semaphores at the crossroads of knowing and oblivion

Mary Lou pardoned by the gods for some hieratic

misstep in the motel of cognition and ecstasy

seasons and weathers gales blizzards and tornados

strife in the cornfields among insect empires haze and heat

rivers flowing sideways into drugstores and ball-games

ricochet and resonance grown hoarse with passion

exulting in the diamond reflux of identity and loss

which are the designations of the prolonged kiss

that dissolves the cosmic snowflake in a madness of light

immense and intolerable love that could not survive

the inane instances of adulthood when all the signals

are missed and memories of grass and stone

and waters blackened by the sun's rippling

AOI

03-18-22

TWO STANZAS ON THE PROPORTION OF DOUBT

i

the reason for writing these poems is first of all

memory is the reason for writing these poems is

love and the –isms attached to the heart's course

for writing these poems is a chaconne a fugue

a folly and a passion for writing these poems is

dual as twins will be on either side of the mirror

which is the reason for writing these poems is death

the only reason for living these poems is dying

these poems is being and nothing and writing more

of these poems is longing to be as before these poems

need writing is death the reason for writing these

poems death is the reason and love's circular

heat and phases of the moon and the divine and
unique moment when these poems were written
dying to the moment when the light was dying
for no reason and stellar signs for writing these
poems is inspiration to die and to be as one with
the other who is writing these poems out of memory
and the song of memory which is the poem being
here and dying to live again the irrevocable moment
for writing these poems without name and no
punctuation and the summer of these poems is
death itself immortal and the boat and the oar
and breath which is the going out and dying again
writing these poems for no reason

ii

great the city and the pain it gives me to realize
we have lived and keep on living in this great city
the university is nearby and the pharmacy and
to realize how much has been lived and even more
how much has died in these recent events as well
as in everything possible in the past of this life
or the lives of others whom we have known or been
can the universe then be so constrained ? knowledge
and information and the disciples of the bleeding moon
the fifth and fourth houses where are they today ?
which of the planets today is the least visible and
which the one that governs the deaths of others ?
to move into the sixth house and linger by the well

where so many calendar dates have drowned can
we then understand ? darkness of the city with
its plenitude of sewers bridges and high-rise dwellings
darkness of this great city where ultimately we must
continue dwelling with its pharmacy and university
and its students who range and roam like lost cattle
or deer grazing the stubble of the hill where dialects
argue the correct form of speech and leave to statues
the essence of being ! blind to the rising and setting
globe of fiery light that travels the sequences of time
and resolves nothing of the fraternal wars and strife
that threaten the airwaves and the links by which
we have learned to breathe without perceiving why
sounds of things that cannot grow and noise and rubble
the bombs that evacuate the heart of memory !

03-19-22

THAT LUCKY OLD SUN

on loan from the gods like moonlight
the ones we grieve the most the lost
or early dead who accompany us as phantoms
could we but hold back the sun's rushing steeds
exchanging that infernal light for the mitigated
lamps of some secluded grove and dally there

in brief deceit for what day's end will always bring
we turn and play and scold and recite in dialect
choice passages of antiquity and hold to the airs
that pass in ignorance promises to maintain
yet lose touch unfold the cloth let spill
the precious bodies that scatter as dust before us
what eyes should never behold nor ear beguiled
should hear the laments and moans of myth
the sorrowing by riverside or dry well
who was it that escaped unobserved in the night ?
our son our brother our friend our mate !
so many who expected to remain on the count
now plunged into the depths somewhere inches
from the mistaken path that leads through gravel
to the midnight bell that never sounds &
today in this world of exploding sirens and hypersonic
missiles directed at the faltering human heart
what mind can be so confused as to congratulate
the sun for rising one more time ?

03-20-22

ON THE EVE OF MEMORY GOING OUT

para mi hermano el único José

corrupted laws of grammar phonetic decay

attrition of sound accumulation of noise

is Sanskrit at war with its own Buddhism

or is it in a struggle with western science ?

Joe , this is the universal question you kept asking

bells toll the inches of heaven fade from prospect

deities immortals gods demons ravage the whole

the fabric is incontinent and colors drain from

the left eye while the right converges with zero

what is the secret formula for transcendence ?

is it one goddess or many who apply opprobrium

to the ear ? *Brother*, were you the pirate or the traveler ?

how far away the grass is where you lost your finger

and the typography of the Greek restaurants

and the evenings spent wasted from some tenuous drug

rooftops scoured the evening shadows for your absence

toiled like dead mariners the abject prisoners

of your love fatal and incongruous to be shared

by the denizens of the world below while in soporific

magnificence you assailed raving the victory of time

the abuse of calendars and notched stone the noon

of everlasting courtship among the statues of bedlam

travesties of language ! the homophone of the gilded globe

lunacy of geminated consonants tongue-twisters

talking in your sleep to the evanescent mother

in her tubercular gown and Mexican amnesia

is all vertigo final ? I ask because only you had

the answer whispering inanities dredged from

the antiquity of our shared boyhood into a plastic device

that carries voices across the millennial seas

from one twin to the other sight unseen and dying

from the tragedy of corporeal tectonics gone wrong

the superficiality of drama and speechifying

stage-fright and aphasia all the words in the lexicon

the enormous Sanskrit volume of a million meanings

and not one so tender as to bear infinity in its longing

++++++++++++++++++++++++++++++++++

there we are on a bridge that crosses the waters of the Lethe

we gaze staring deep into the invisible worlds

of the unremembered and pledge to keep our hearts clean

so that some time in the future of the letter Rho

we will recall how we lived those few brief seasons

on planet earth's streets and rectangles and bluffs

looking for always searching but never really finding

Brother, were you the pirate or the traveler ?

03-21-22

THE UNHEARD VOICE
José Argüelles in memoriam

comes a time when all calendars die

moment of universal change when

numbers sums and ciphers lose their firmament

in the second grade we learned all we needed

to know about counting and in the twelfth grade

we learned there was nothing in between

number two and number three but

an excess of space and unfathomable direction

maps of cities enormous plans of diachronic structures

pyramids with the value of seventy two years

does anything exist beyond the borders of light

or is there no substitute for memory?

there we were straddling the hill of radiance

and discomposure everything at a stand-still

as eternity tends to be and heat the sun's homophone

and the finely knitted air of catastrophe and death

puzzling as ever over the function of pronoun and mask

person and obligation the near-future like a crime

that must be committed and our own selves slaves

to destiny unwritten and fruitless as its conjecture may be

you alone pronounced some forbidden syllables

and together we practiced the languages of antiquity

exchanging the rhombus and buzz of etymology

for the vibration and meaning of sounds alone

and in a wink centuries passed and on a street corner

in San Francisco we embraced and wept

knowing we would never again force the hand

of grammar and swept away by some invisible divinity

you passed the line of demarcation of breath and sight

and we parted forever on parallel trajectories

that may someday come together again

if numbers sums and ciphers regain their firmament

03-22-22

JOE

it's all too unbearable

the weight of light

the circumference of memory

the short circuit of breath

the empty mirror

why was I not there

to touch and feel

the way you went

to hear your voice

going out to space

to watch your eyes

conclude their trace

why did I not know

you were about to race

some errant star

to its resting place

together we used to lie

in the self same bed

and recite unknown words

in a Mexican dialect

akin to pyramids and suns

brothers in a secret

realm of page and sound

fingers of ink and grass

books of echoing air

rivulets we drank

to become something else

no one would ever ken

alone and apart

you took your body

on a fevered route

that kept me out

to this day I cannot be

the whole I was

when I was with *Thee*

03-22-22

THE DISCOURSE ON HISTORY

is world history determined

by religion or by language ?

are the ten Directions governed

not by deities but demons ?

repetition resonance and vibration

what else but sound can have meaning ?

other ways to cross the River

have been refuted by the Letter

unseen crimes committed in dark groves

are witnessed by sun and moon alike

too many planets have plunged

before their time unassailed unlamented

the cyclotron like the Church of England

both inventions of the Fiend !

why go on with poetry of make-believe

mythology of cognition and

rock formations as dualities

to be considered when smashing

the atom in order to resolve conflict

how many times have we been here

prattling on about judgment and

consciousness the daylight

that absorbs the half of youth

in a riot of escapade and emotion

driving vehicles over futile cliffs

or draining the mouth with kisses

stolen when literature isn't looking

to map the great pyramids that

establish the mind's polarities

going to sleep embraced

to an empty body and to wake !

when was that an option ?

gathered as we are in this funnel

dominated by darkness and intuition

who of us is really the *other*

and who the unmentionable ?

earth is a wobbling toy

about to self-destruct

the writings of the past !

cannibals and pygmies strutting

with pride on buffalo skulls

look again at the photo

the kid three fingers from the right

is dead !

a Greekling derided by the gods

dipped in diesel fuel and left

to consider his quandary burning

nevermore scream the headlines

yet tomorrow is here

with still another explosive

military operation

Buddha-nature is not militant

it is washing the feet

of those who have traveled

far from home and birthright

it is learning to sleep

next to the empty body

below eons of indifferent space

filled with noise

it is abandoning the pronoun

and destroying the mask

we have all been characters

in a drama without a plot

a blade of grass

the dark season

memory

03-23-22

ANCIENT DRAMA

mistaken coaches horses of the sun

traipsing the royal-way unheeded

pronoun in distress pitch-black

incantations of the muse and longing

distraction of magic and jewelry

like vast splendors of the unwritten

word the unheard note the crescendo

of the universe that neighbors ours

cosmos of intellect and submission

the various characters acting parts

of adolescent and queen garlands

worn all around and inserted vowels

that take the place of effigies copies of

ancient rulers of the underworld whose

anger and volubility to behold are glory

ruminating on the sacred texts which

cluster consonants on the divide and loud

phraseologies of the sun the violent

metal that holds sleep back from its

unformed dreams of language and what

takes place between allusions to the moon

speeches whispered into a marble ear

gravel and glass and music of drum

and tambourine hooves of beasts

known for their antiquity maze of

corollaries about the youth of time and

evermore the floral bouts and debates

of love and disconsolation in small

volumes of unutterable verse efforts

of the eyes to bind man's frail hope

to distances beyond ken and whatever

stage the playwright demands wave

and grief of early deaths bells tolling

in silent spheres of grassy twilight

today ! cremation and syllogism isogloss

of the fatal hand archetype of the void

today ! memory the devouring flame

brother's role played out at last

03-24-22

STAGES OF LIFE

famous and fabulous the houses of the sun

no less worthy of oblivion the lunar mansions

stages of life ! there are women like islands

who wear one hundred gold bracelets on each arm

and have hair so strong as to defy typhoons

it's all conjecture and siphon in the drugstore

high-school yearbooks in fading cuneiform

photos of everyone who ever existed !

everything has already happened and

will never happen again not here nor on Mars
evenings when the trade-winds exchange hotels
for mausoleums and crematoria and sun-bursts
so beautiful you want to drive off the cliff and
join the movie with Natalie Wood and James Dean
waking and listening to music from the year 1616
Monteverdi and Cervantes and the Turkish surgeon
dialing an invisible cipher to get in touch with
the corn fields and heat-storms and cicadas
going wild inside a mortuary of glass and alcohol
no one has ever lifted off from this extra-planetary
hour and survived to tell about it unless
asleep and reciting discourse on right thinking
the syntax of leaf and stone and summers mirrored
in the collapse of memory and so much more or less
the staggered conventions of thought and trance
each of us riddled with the notion of escape
and salvation and the waters rising to take the knees
and the scalpel of reason driving from right to left
and the hairline and buzzwords of the intellect
come to a standstill in the reversed moment of eternity
looking back ! I was never there I never did anything
the hill and its obscure dialect of accident and dance
folios of wasted Latin declensions the black-board !
counting backwards in Italian until there are no more numbers
returning the body to the unremembered depths of sleep
which shirt will I wear today ?

will my brother wear the same shirt ?

03-25-22

ONCE I HAD A SECRET LOVE

a time when the universe couldn't exist
simplicity of noise and silence without form
and sense the abracadabra of pre-existence
when no mother's womb avails and space
is a distant copy of sleep and inert arms
embrace the enormous lack of consciousness
do we come from such unknown origins ?
light seeping in under the lintel of cognition
and stars and tigers and the mountain-tops of thought
lessons to be learned in word formations lingering
in the long doubt of afternoons in a chalk-storm
act of creation in rock and stubble gravel and
grassy patches and shepherds dreaming cities
murals and seas passing through a tiny cipher
circular weathers and high-school dictations
in a language that cannot be taught
no wonder hesitation and anguish dominate
fearing to touch the telephone and dial a number
and the lunations all twenty-eight in a sudden spark
somewhere to the right of the sky's northwest quadrant

epiphanies of daylight in the revolving windows
of the Mayo Clinic aspersions of the occident
even as the girls in their plaid pinafores chatter on
about the daily evolution and trees that stop to consider
in which direction the love supreme lies!
leaf and ivy stucco walls like Mycenaean inscriptions
and learning to use motors and turn the wheels of destiny
music in a hidden convent of the record store
details and minutiae of the secret conversation
with the deity of immobility and hills resonating
with the radio's top forty songs of the week
and if there are at least two or three other universes
tumbling malignantly outside the borders of known light
and planets with no egress bearing the names of humans !
imagine the confusion of adolescence extended
to the tombstone moldering beside the abandoned motel
where Jupiter once held assignations with mortals
kill and joy of the hunt ! Diana ! reading from
the footnotes of a discarded Latin text she looms
sinister and shadowy despite the lamps
following our every step to the Senior Prom
and with whom she chooses to dance !
the boy whose body remains forever unidentified

03-26-22

BREATHLESS

the cosmos ! spectacular inch of light that

radiates backwards to the time of our birth

hospitals and snowstorms and lawns of oblivion

a single street paved with gravity that separates

the unknown from the unknown ! dandelions

plucked from the entrance to hell and gasoline

extending its peninsula into graduation day

the four divided by two and the violent gamma

rays of the endless numeral three like a cathedral

of mind and intersections of beauty and thought

who was the Greek boy dragged under by fate's

irrevocable wheel that dateless Sunday in spring ?

the alternate infinity of memory is riddled with

spurious conclusions to grass and galaxies spinning

out of control the device won't turn off the thrum

and drone of a cellular music in the ear of sleep

haunted we will always be by the first cigarette

and the way the older girl eyed us introducing us

to flamenco and the splendors of India's far western

province Spain and imitations of shadow and flight

bees swarming on the trestle that bridges poetry

mountains ! how fast speaking in dialect the landscape

alters its afternoon eternity as we drive vessels of

pure stream into the cornfields heralding the day

when we will no longer need shirts and brilliant

effigies of red and hair the size of Japan and sweat

falling into the first of many grammars an account

of a vision when the twin pyramids of sun and moon

held us momentarily dead before taking the plunge

from the present tense into the future darkness

lack of pronouns ! statues suffering aphasia and

deaf to the wants of justice and fame how much more ?

03-27-22

DELIRIUM OF LIGHT

whenever I see kids age eight nine or ten

gleefully cavorting on an empty school ground

or hear a mourning dove hidden in foggy grey

with its coded lament for someone just taken by the gods

and when I see some grassy lawn echoing noisily

with sounds of make-believe in a city of never-was

far from the reaches of ancient galactic storms

so great unknown and empty the world seems

and I stop to wonder looking all around the sky

who then is riding that ambulance to eternity ?

when I see spaceships the size of plastic toys

scattered in the darkest spatial quarters where

unseen stars go when they've lost their spark

and wherever I walk there's no place that the cosmos

does not resonate a lost boyhood that came and went

not being registered by the librarian of games

is it that the turning earth is just not there

and events that seem to have occurred so loud

and vivid are only fragments glimpsed in a troubled sleep ?

dream-schemes hands undone long unpunctuated summers

fading photographs that clutter the grasping mind

images distracted poles of flame and rain windows

that give way to maps of surrendered breath

the intermittent fever that finally won the day

in this sleep within the sleep of depths it's Max

looking for another way to Wednesday afternoon

there do angels speak in hieroglyphs waving vast hands of sand

in their eyes huge deserts die thirsting for the light

they come to tell me of redundancy and fate

I listen but hear nothing more than a thin voice

from as far away as the mountains of the moon

relating incidents from basement stores of a former life

echolalia and dialect of long unspoken love

blades of grass leaves stained with tears

small moments not lived just imagined

in the labyrinth of time

03-28-22

ERROR AND RUMOR

it's only because of language that we err

so frequently with such rumor and noise

there are valleys we don't understand

do we know which is the last hill to reach the sun ?

can we really be sure of ourselves ?

there are so many ways to die

and what about caves and grottos

and the myth that mountains can fly ?

memory is the always incomplete dimension

if it were whole would we need to live ?

fragments of a shattered mirror is what

we remember going through topographies

and incidental music and the many accidents

language is no way to get through this labyrinth

of sound and noise meaningless interruptions

of light and thought we gather one hand

and hold it high to some kind of standard

that includes flight and cognition of the abyss

only to leave the other in an obfuscation

of ceremony and ritual never knowing which

is the right and which is the left in this dream

of sequences and parallels reflections left over

from adolescence and the impression

that grammar will eventually correct itself

great motor vehicles ! images and copies

of speed and gravity and luminescence

when will this aggravated day ever end ?

repetition of hours confusion of calendar dates

aging without responsibility and the chairs

and vacuum cleaners and moveable pieces

of energy and thunder ultimately and yes

windows ! to look and observe nothing

but the factory of clouds ready to burn

wars ! incognito pronouns of literature !

and how we speak and what we say

talking as if verbiage had content and statues

effigies and corollaries imaginary histories

listen to me ! I love you !

03-29-22

SLEEP'S LUCID CONFUSION

others have died and me too

on the threshold between space

and its alternate oblivion

time past when burning

and adolescence were the same

and witness to glass and light

growing up insensate to

situations of air and clouds

whole eternities in a simple

summer afternoon at the pool

listening not hearing shouts

and jibes mushrooming in

the recycled heat of memory

learning to sleep in that riot

of perplex and feigned silence

imagination which is the mind

working furiously to conjure

lovers and hospital beds

a future of sorrow and acrimony

disbelief in contours of the moon

kept awake nights by rumors

of death in the floor-boards

asking of what is oblivion made

the second and third days

of the voyage to southland

where the recent dead

puzzle over the use of hands

and feet and mimic the parrot

in its cage of abstract flame

voices words sonant glyphs

the running water of error

that pours through the ear

trajectories of sand and oil

can anything ever return

to the condition before sound ?

writing comes into being

in the fraction of time that

it takes to fall asleep

and enormous conjectures

of origins and endings

of the cosmos on the shores

of an illiterate sea and

to scribble these thoughts

on a slate of air darkening

like the metaphor of cognition

as it comes and goes in a flash

hidden by the sun's black

and distant homophone

03-30-22

PERSEPHONE – AN EPIPHANY

wearing a head-dress of peacock feathers

studded with emeralds sapphires and jade

the goddess of all things that fade appeared

to us clad in dust ghosting avenues of parallel

cities disunited unwholesome lost and weary

to the bone and yet her splendid smile shone

a brief instant making us believe for that gap

in time that immortality was within hand's reach

whatever lay behind the lost hills we sought

to re-create as if memory could be turned into

matter manifest or statuary to behold whenever

how deep was the crevice between our passage

and the *underworld* where she returned to speak

to the already evanescent gods the others who

pass into the gloaming as planets glamorous

for their weight and speed and we mere earthlings

most of us already dead in the space of the minute

when adolescence and shining metal combine

to make a catastrophe and intermittent sleep

and redundancies of recall and error overwhelm

us unconscious denizens of pale spirit worlds

sound and traffic plate-glass reflections of motion

gravity and distance mountains of oblivion

the utter end-all of existence in a torn leaf and airs

and clouds and bitumen and pitch the densities

of inferno surround us ghosting offices and condos

matching and mismatching pronouns insufferable

ego-play over cocktails and rumors pounding fists

of insomnia on the rooftop watch for the stars

just what do we think this masquerade is all about ?

lay the heavy head on a dark patch of grass waiting

for stone and gravel to emit signals of salvation

our disembodied voices at prayer for the goddess

of all things that fade to reappear just once again

and deliver our remains to the vast and shadowy

netherworld where she reigns mysteriously absent

03-31-22

ALEPH

breath becomes circular searching for heat the liaison

body at will subsides next to the bone wall separating

this world from the other one described in the manual

as the Counting House where angels submit blindly

nothing coherent everything random chaos aflame

mind a series of incomprehensible word shots

flicker tape black and white unfinished dreams un-

ending silence followed by the primordial Shout!

who woke up who started running who learned to write

the alphabet first who went face down in the flowers

who remembered nothing all over again the red brick
street many ancient books countless unwritten pages

the spirit world is just millimeters off our skin
a halo of imperceptible breath on the leaf

03-31-22

SO LET'S BEAT THE DRUM AND
REPEAT THE PROCLAMATION !

all this talk of cremation grounds and heaven
condemned souls liberation at last salvation
in the playwright's hand ink and pen a paper
that weighs nothing about to fly with the winds
of yesteryear and all that too a speech set in stone
gravel and glass the garden left to seed overgrown
moss and weed and ivy can one see so far and
still forget the final moment and set forth a trip
between battered rock and seas unknown a script
to learn by daybreak and night-sounds stars and
asterisks and glorious forgotten words snatches
of noise like pearls of music mirrors and stairs
and cigarette smoke in the vestibule adolescents
learning grammar to recite lines anew and loves

and perfumes and darkened thoughts to have and
lose at once in passions the shadowy and fleeting
dream between libraries and drugstores and
bells that toll the recent dying and to fling sand
in the face of some truant god whose duty is
to assail setting up ropes and clinics and snows
that storm the winter memory of being *there*
was once ever enough to be born and pass the
waning day in sunset hills of melancholy longing
and adversaries of the underworld with tongs
and hammers and nails praising the Messiah
whose vindication never comes the streets are
filled with sleep and the smaller maps indicate
there is nowhere else to go but death's errant
crib the rumor of a Masonic dance and sections
of sunlight scattered across deserted cornfields
a highway that comes and goes and depths
to celebrate the moment lived and never more
remember what has to be remembered

04-01-22

ASTOLFO ON THE MOON

other ponds other streams other rivers
somewhere else a valley between two
unknown mountains where years are
hidden like heaps of gold and sorrow
is the very shadow *haunted by negativity*
compass and fingernail histories of dust
underground canals and fine tooth-combs
elements of a world beyond time a fix
in the arm a rodeo of ghostly caravanserais
tumult of sleep in the second hour of eternity
what can be more infinite than yesterday ?
declensions of light vague presentiment
that some of this has happened before and
may occur again at the junction of memory
and mimesis outside the range of hearing
where nymphs who are copies of earthly ones
chase wild beasts of the archaic across sterile
mine-fields and plateaus of mental ash
there is no looking back no staring into
the mirror's recondite identity nor reading
the oriental script erased with every dawn
epoch of horses extravagant for their absence
and rutilations of pedigreed stars comma and
ink-blot of galaxies revolving soundlessly

in the movie theater of youth where Orlando

struggles with his own pronominal madness

and Angelica is a flight of conditional wings

luxury and luminescence of distant portraits

lunations of infinite redundancies nothing

is ever what it appears to be apocrypha and

language reverberating in the small chasm

the exit from the moon annunciation

and vertigo archetype and enigma

hieroglyphs of oblivion

remember the sun !

04-02-22

POST-MORTEM

> *" my br'Other*
>
> O. Lindsann, *Arthur Dies*, v. 5

I am my brother's afterlife float and breath
heart and leaf sound and echo vertigo and death
me I'm always front and center second from the left
trying to figure ways in and out of his fourth dimension
going up the smoking ladder leading to the shelf-life
of the letter zed and when I've finished counting
all the numbers between the rose and its hundredth hue

night revolves its tendrils inside my inner ear and
I hear all the eons since time began written in *italics*
and the boom and surf of endless seas the lights
that make planets err the horizons on the other side
of space so much left to understand but lack the buzz
and burr of intellect to comprehend the whole and list
from side to side half of what I should have been
hospitals like space-ships give birth to memory
and who he might have been presides wavering
for a moment only before he quits the poem that
I am writing in the air a flute of noises a hand of sounds
etches from a golden horn and peninsulas of glyphs
such strange clamor in a water made of shadows
and grasses more plentiful than depth come running
to take us by the knees at play with childhoods
that derive their eternities from the enigmas
we mapped in the noon of our brief morning life
just think what he would say today as I stretch
the myth of letters from space dark mists
that have no resonance no form nor statue other
than the missing light the chance to play and fail
grammar's obscure linearity and renunciation
which begins at the top of the Book darkling
signs grimoire and testamentum doubled by
our twisted paths up and down the final hill
ovations in ears of stone passionately devoted

to the monogram and its queen at the height

where Lorca and Rimbaud unencumbered drown

in the raindrop that destroyed Troy and what's

more *dear Bro'* the edge is never sanctified and

though I trouble the left shoulder more than the right

I try not to look back at all the unfinished paintings

the murals scrapped at the last minute sunsets

and muted dawns with their epistolary horses

that bring no truce to the muted appeals of death

to have it out in backlands where dialects

turn to sand and bracken weir quiet fusion

of a late jazz afternoon with its peyote horizon

stoned and amazed at the futility of life depicted

in the mind's imagined trespass of breath and

autumns ! crashing silently on the other side of sleep

so long, Man, you done it whether good or bad

but you done it on your own stage-play and left

me here to be twice what I can never be alone

04-03-22

YET ANOTHER APRIL

Whan that Aprille with his shoures soote,
April is the cruelest month
when did everything happen ?
we were just kids then coming to know
the fragile gravity of air and
the indispensible weight of light
the periodic chart only explained half
of the understood content of matter
the rest was in the inevitable paradise
of longing in the eyes of a passing nymph
what was the name of the dark city
we were bidden to enter unawares ?
every day was the last day of the world
poetry and grammar spokes on a wheel
turning constantly from noon to midnight
nights were salvaged for a brief
moment of cognition and love
but who was the Host and who
the inexplicable Archetype who stood
at the foot of the bed ?
it's all so unbearable this burning
that moves its flame from day to day
memory splinters into two million and
one fragments like a kaleidoscope
colored bits of shattered jewelry
who is who and which is which

that claims to be the *other*?
lists of rotations and redundancies
drugs-store counters with perfumes
plate-glass reflections and mobility
stolen cars bridges and great rivers
dreams of becoming angels with combs
stylized skin and speech of stone
cannon and magistrates of the hour
nothing can be pieced together
leaf and tumult of hills in dialect
talking incessantly to the book
of missing pages and making up
travels to Yucatan and 4th dimension
high on alert the brain receives
signals from an unknown source
histories and chronologies of water
invasion from northern languages
and troubadours of amnesia
adolescence and the tribe of
poets and magicians who
have altered the course of time
acts of prestidigitation and howls
on and on the discoveries and
failures of alcohol and speed
how few of us remain here *now*?
laid to rest put out of mind
forgot the name but not the face

04-04-22

THE REST OF MY LIFE

    what does it mean

  the rest of my life ?

is there anything more archaic

than the hoe that tills the garden soil

that turns the worm that fuels the blood

that rushes through the working arm ?

eyes that are facets of the sun and poetry

that stirs wordlessly beneath the skin

budding branch flowering air

language that has no relative in the realm

of senses and haunted *others* that move

and shift in the precarious inches

that surround the imagined body of the self

egos and pronouns of the honorific style

to pursue just one of the myriad tangled threads

that lead from the unfinished page to

the unaltered and tumultuous seas of Homer

blessing and curse both to *remember*

knowing the past is an inevitable futility

that can never be correctly recovered

but *the rest of my life ?*

how many cities does that make on the road-map

that lies crumpled in some back lot ready to burn ?

the child ! the unutterable specter of joy

followed by the canker sore of bewilderment

the lost summers the hospital rooms

the lovers who call in agony out of the welter

and rumor of the world's disease and heat

and the perpetuity of air and bridges

that simply dangle incomplete over the waters

that darken with every passing moment

to read into the mind's puzzle of grammar

a sort of lexicon of order and continuity

what greater error is there than that !

what is recalled other than snatches of

conversation cafes now boarded up friends

signaling with echoes to a vaster significance

that cannot be deciphered and streets and engines

hills and brooks meadows with spotted deer

relics of the Buddha in the broken tiles

where shadows walk looking for a name

the *rest of my life* but a faulty reconstruction

of a passage through sleep brief

and illusory but a transient moment

confused dream of an orient

I'll never reach

04-04-22

HOMERIC FRAGMENT

'til day's end we spent sorting out the waves

water by water in the ink-swell of torment

storms of the purpled west rising hemispheres

of air permeated with dust-globes the swart sun

high and immobile without recall and cast lots

soul given to soul and agony of thought the thin

membrane that separates from death the living

to breathe in miasma and fortitude alike and

sighted from afar the sheer cliff of distance lifting

a hand dropping the oar a splash resounding like

language unspoken among the electrified fishes

that swarm the mind jettisoned orders flung

and winds sudden shift turning cold from the

heated rays on our backs purposeless the mast

against the heaving columns of rain dense and

adrift the remainder of the hour waiting for a

deity to give us shrift and no more blinded than

the statues of an incomplete memory the signals

fingers of stars plucked from the sky's darkening

quarter and still we circled the eddying rifts crazed

lips cracked the bole and thrust of sculpted oak

oracle and voice drilling the ear the terrific buzz

born in the abandoned hills beloved of mortals but

now set by lugubrious fate yellowing clay that we

men are and symbols of red and slattern escape

of ideas to round the infirmities of decision harsh

cloying arm against foil to sleep if possible winding

the spool of cognition who could hear the secret

whispering of madness the goddess it was who

with recoil and gorgeous in her luster of skin

pearled with *enigmas* to whom appeared and sent

among tide and essence of salt reeking of wine

depths set to quarrel for possession as if dice

tossed on the flayed skin tanned in the augury of

heat and to one another desperately glanced eyes

sparked with smoldering rage quick to knife

illusions how could then day's end come about

without shed blood the quoits of aggravation

each his own wave and to drown seeing above

the bird of mystery great span of wings shadowy

covering the light and sounds mourning the cry

of sorrow who of us gone so quickly the thread

snapped and watching the gurgling liquids foam

blood-tainted and agony the noise of vanishing

04-05-22

PROSERPINA'S COUNTING-HOUSE

"Hos iuxta falso damnati crimine mortis"

Aeneid, VI, 430

does one come to be dead unscathed ?

mutilated mauled the thought of skin

offered to a god unknown the wastes

excoriated light living in the past a final

wafer of kindled energy spirit sent aloft

the host of blind angels scratching sky

for a cloud weft organization of memory

for whom the candles and sputtering

in the rare film of fading air the end

so near at day night takes by the knees

folding shadows until they disappear

hills and cloisters that grieve the soul

gone unnoticed the window's open glare

asleep fell elbow to mouth a softening

dream of grass bending under weight of

dark the thin flare of stars passing into

attic of memory dusky wings suspended

because day is no more but a lack of

vowels a shivering in the ear a smaller

gravity descending with the noise of

frogs and crickets in the counting-house

astray from right thinking the body's

immateriality if it could choose language

to soar expression and flaw alike bound

to the hand and what singular event

fingers that explore the next life's sound

ancient ! flux of waters beneath sorrow

the lament of rooms that darken each

lingering like smoke without doorways

and the steps careful to ascend silence

metaphor and symbols of waning sun

passage to other worlds exits and comb

density of hair a fullness in the palm

noise of waves going under towing

reflections and the idiom of stress

loud in the stone heavy the head shift

of tones and missing the bow a flank

wounded hidden deities in the leaf

aiming and roar of bee-swarm the ear

capsized thus and enter Proserpina's

limitless depths unfelt and forever

04-05-22

THE MYSTERY OF LANGUAGE

it is time for Hera and Athena to shake hands

put an end to the war of sounds to the shattering

paraphernalia of noise combat of dust and air
placing definition before meaning and the riot
& helter-skelter of mortals in constant combat
over a supernal syllable snatched out of ear-shot
goddesses in disarray where forest meets river
stone and labyrinthine mind imperfect memory
of horse-taming and the irreverent hush before
the storm and skies turned multiple and fierce
nowhere to sleep with good conscience nowhere
the right burial with indistinct symbols decaying
phonetics glyphs uttered without regard to shape
pictograms of echo vibrating in pre-dawn flare
to capture the singular consonant and match it
with the panoply of vowels and call that sacred
mustering futility against futility to make under-
standing more than a hand-gesture or a bone
preserved for its quantity and the burr in the throat
the zzing and roar of bee swarms in summer heat
the turn of a leaf making it holy and the hum and
whir the bilateral and dubious first cluster of
a conscious articulation to designate and name
I am here! there is thunder in the wind there
are notable spirits called trees and flowers
that represent the birth of gods that can never
be seen and soon we will be in hand to hand
combat over the unseen border dividing yours
from mine and pronouns will be invented for

exultation and the descriptions of deeds outside
of recollection and counting as high as three before
feuding over the value of a fist and a thumb if
that is five ! so many things occur at once and
smoke especially how to hold it and shape it
fire which must be kept infinite and rock and sand
the foot-hold on a cliff waves of angry waters
spots in the heavens at night burning and shaking
someone says it is poetry to remember !
the first poet is blind and knows nothing about
the versions of light that shatter and often kill
knows even less about the vanity of creating
there are quarrels over pronunciation and meter
fixities of tone evaluations of meaning lightning
broad thoroughfares grottos secret wells deaths
depths in the sockets of atmosphere where souls
are said to go flying wingless and weightless
mystery of language ! it is the descendants
of poets who destroy it with ego display who
have forgotten the flight-formation of birds
or the enigma of hills where the sun disappears
and that a day is no day at all but a remnant
of eternity a statue of the invisible and unheard
it is time for Hera and Athena to shake hands

04-06-22

A TWIN'S TALE

"Only a fadograph of a yestern seene."
             Finnegans Wake

once numb but too dumb to tell the tale

twice told of twins oft declined in spells

of light and airy bluster height and fold

of steps to climb mastery of both moon

and sun in stone and glyph the bright

in Greek fading heart signs and sounds

the cold war culture's gone ashes split

between Toynbee and Spengler under

going the west in sequence of shattered

frieze mural scope distant hills soughing

discord among heliotrope and daisy

what flowers may sleeping brains display

of old and rope the hands that bind a

swaying dance a smoke as cold as wines

that oft spill do dialects dispose a *The*

cancelled playing the pliant mind's

choice game a hare a hind the hilly

slope down slide the which is we again

reborn this morn a springtime sprint

memory's colloidal sea some poetry

rhymed backwards to sides to brace

sings one the other's grace a page

bent back to reveal stone ampersand

and attics sleeping still the wings tilt

toward some other dawn lace of slight

lamps that rill the foaming brook under

beds that roll from top to silt river's

sedge wick and reed movie-reel wrack

and ruin shadows doubled in their stead

what ! brings ho and fills the shovel with

granny's soil digs deeper delves death

what's more unsaid the entranced ear

whose *echo* is now the unseen finger

left yearning in the twilight grass

04-06-22

LA SELVA OSCURA

what is to wake when sleep brings its own

devastations rock and salt the mire and dense

hills which none may pass but for the voices

whirring in dark air and dreams half-spent

color drained from clouds and the eye cast

about for hues to maintain some shape or

form of being would day the next differ in

any sense recalling the hum and drone naiads

hiding in an eddying tumult of waters swirl

of memory and green depths where the hand
searched for its other in a stage-play of riot
and royal melancholy the head bruited sounds
if words snatched from the reveries could
make sense the tales told in their wake a
height and winds bearing secret deities of
leaf and arbor vine and moss peering between
interstices of light and breath great spaces
uncountable moments recollections of dance
in motion the slender spires of noise swaying
bodies no longer feel mind thrust into void
so much and so little left to revive and nerve
and asterisk punctuation for lack of order
about when and where only the grief louder
than remembered shadow and shallows in
woods labyrinthine and brotherless pounding
hoof and drum ear to the pierced trunk dry
in the middle of the air and dull glaring
unexpectedly the black sun risen from behind
the left shoulder and posing for a group photo
the class inaugurates its spate of mask and
pronoun before night sets in again with its
grammar of insomnia chaos and echo

04-07-22

MY ALMOST FAMOUS FATHER /
MY LONG-SUFFERING MOTHER

"Survivors include ... two sons, Ivan of
Berkeley, Calif., and José of South America ..."
  from the obit of Enrique Argüelles,
    Entered into Eternal Rest, Dec. 5, 1994

chaotic dance of memory reconstructions of echo
glossolalia in Spanish Braille jargon of fingers
released from suffering disorder and early sorrow
include a grandson who also died previously
and the paraphernalia of noise that accompanies
pride and discomfort art on its own career
through multiple schemes of winter and melancholy
longing for the day the Zapatistas rode into town
and marrying exactly ten years before the birth
of the twins one of whom claims as residence
an entire continent from Iguazu falls to Chichen Itza
if it weren't for the mosaics in a nunnery nor
for the long nights jumping a scrabble board
nor for the two year stay in tuberculosis ward
if it weren't for Mexico City itself loud Aztec
charnel house with infernal police and assassination
of great Communist thinker and Coyoacán
home to demonic painters and Nahuatl coyotes
how else explain the mysterious and cosmic
lives of the two sons orthographically misplaced

consumed by solar and lunar trajectories mapped
and discarded repeatedly in the emerging noosphere
and Mom naïve in her spirituality and pathos
Friday nights waiting for everyone to come home
despite alcohol and infidelity and inexplicable music
the murals ! automobile tires and cheap cocktails
religion in every brush stroke and the sound of geese
flying through seasons of intense nostalgia
nothing was ever the same and nothing was ever
really correct despite the thunder and the avenues
of heat and the swimming through lozenges of despair
and Mom just sitting there waiting out midnights
gasoline and dusty country roads and resonance
in German dialect of darkness and elimination
cemeteries and lakes ! borderline madness every day
secrets of annihilation and great art mispronounced
while spreading out designs of the celestial lawn
willow and plum trees white stucco and nights
that belong only to automobiles and gravel
for Mom "there will be no visitation or services"
just the opaque redundancies of living in two languages
unflawed Mayo Clinic Spanish and high school English
the children who were reared in violence and aesthetics
gone their separate careers a daughter twin sons
alphabets of broken narration lexicons of distance
for Enrique "the funeral will be private" the artist

who was once Lázaro Cárdenas' right-hand man
and later created a floor-screen with baroque motifs
for Mrs Charles Mayo who was pleased and excited
to display this work of art

04-08-22

THE DESERTED SCHOOLYARD OF MEMORY

the broken heart quaking and in the dim
air branches just budding moved by the violence
of thought and encumbrances pale distances
shaking that no eye can hold the past with
its marble effigies half in ruin an old man's voice
trembling to recall admitting once *life is great*
the days wander aimlessly into the tunnel
that leads to the woods of oblivion and a signal
from the gathering dusk wings heard fluttering
prognostications of the mind's oncoming night
as memory slowly winds down of the meadow
and the small dappled deer at the entrance
waiting for a rebirth a kindling of ancient
flames on an altar turned to dust nuances of echo
in the ricocheting waters unseen rushing below
a mythical rock fragment and the smell of

newly washed hair the naiads looking for

the sun on their polished stone of evidence

not even the sound of the ancient wind arrives

all at a standstill in the imperfect moment when

waking is more enigmatic than ever and the flush

of ruddy dawn held just far enough away

no one can hear precisely what the old man's

voice is trying to say the recital of a mantra

from the time when plum trees blossomed

scraping hieroglyphic limbs against the stucco

darkness everywhere dispersing its vowels

the broken heart the deer nibbling the edges

rumor of light half-ruined marble effigies

memory in its final manifestation beneath

the sky's immense and inexplicable shadow

04-09-22

"SIGHTLESS NARRATION"

Pound

so close to the sunlit path but

never made it to where is brighter

air less the cloud-warp book of songs

from the first by rock and glade

to make music midst dandelions

underbrush cry of the rooks circling

in the meridian of heat a chance to

understand the sounds crickets and

frogs and romantic preludes in the winds

thorn and abscess of mind but to travail

against the atmospheres and sudden

as thunder in the sun's back vowel

face down in turf and listening

for the hollow palm to echo nymph's

clear voice will come to naught soon

at hour's end on the needle and heart-

spun aching in circular dismay was

once here beside the image a copy of

something seen in a dream read in

a text pursued to no avail to remember

and write the experienced moment

is greater the thought the less it

can articulate but vague and strange

presentiment that it may happen

but not again and the woods to the side

the labyrinth the unknown passage

to get out of this life to the other one

were it not forgetting how to proceed

verbs and descriptors that ply the dusky

light and hills barely perceived

the language of poetry hidden in them

afternoon's waning promise and

soon the chill of night

as snow that clings to evergreens

04-10-22

PHANTOM HELEN

what did I call her in my sleep

my princess ! my goddess ! slut !

noise of the brain's disorder to summon

phantoms from uncommon summer heat

a year that took an hour one afternoon to complete

the ships caulked and repaired to set sail

by morn dewfall and watch of time

wave-length and unbidden darkness

the radio's voice stuffed with static and plying

the shore long ells of despond and memory

of the tower surface of light an end to night

among glazed galaxies where speech is

conveyed as electricity a stage-play

with masks and mummers mufflers and goldenrod

held hand-high in the school performance

darker the lessened background changing

clothes like skin the gleaming swart edge

of metal and the pliant air of curtains dense

as lessons of rhetoric grammar and math

one by one watched them drop from breath

in the gloomy stillness beneath the garden

out-back next to the garage and the whetstone

in the gloaming dusk of statues fingers

digging deeper to retrieve the shadow if possible

moaning in the leaves whose tribulations

and twittering like bats in the attic where

surmise and intent are planned as strategy

miles to go before Troy and the surrounding seas

waters of rebuff and oriental chaos

Helen bound for Egypt before the next whistle

and armor askew sand and gravel fistfuls

tossed at the blackened window of the sun

lamp-wick and soot smudging fingertips

that delve and strive to spell her names

vibrating in the already archaic winds lifting

above Cretan outlines afloat a dream

chance and spur of identity upon waking

empty bed sheets yellowed from perspiration

her it was the shape dissolute in linens

now the vanished twilight tangent

a bird a mystery a form of language that

cannot bend to the rules sonant as gold

burnished in remembrance of the other time

lofty Mycene with its stone lions

mists now arabesques of sleep

04-10-22

THE CRY IN THE WOOD
HEARD BY NO ONE

who is that crying in the wood

at this steep hour in these dark depths ?

a voice from the heart a distance of tears

a grimace last seen in rooms forbidden to light

an echo winnowing in unfathomable air

night-winds and scales falling from unseen spheres

the planets and their assigned numbers circling

without design in the canvas of galaxies burning

with insignia of death before their time

immensities of sleep riddled with ghosts

mnemonic structures syntax of mythic seasons

swells of water reflecting green embroidery of leaf

among clouds the lesser celestial mysteries moon

and irrevocable comets and missiles sent by gods

portents of ire and pest plans for war and siege

laying multiplied cities to rest beneath flames of thought

dust and panoplies of heat and machines

riot of silence and despair in the labyrinth

but who is that crying in the wood ?

somber lesions that discolor forecasts of birth

hands reconfigured to grasp things unheard

to wake but only in a dream of waking

and gaze upon shorelines aggregates of rock and

sculpted marble and listen to the hue and cry

plazas and myrmidons and shield-bearing mortals

fragments of poetry half-uttered words

torn from a script and characters shadowy

and in motion yet struggling with curtain and mask

pronouns ! crying in the wood for someone

or something a recollection a drug a spindle

gravity of afternoons trying to learn a speech

hills and diameters of lamplight cast before dusk

circularity of mind ! talk of going forth

to seek new lands and languages that confound

assigning names to objects that separate

life from life such as javelin or grenade

tossed carelessly against the wind

victims everywhere as is the lot of man

stoned corrupted in the futile passage

through but never out of the wood

a drum in the ear and recoil of thunder

smaller still the voice crying in the wood

muffled or drowned in the unpunctuated sleep

of a cosmos without beginning

04-11-22

DE SENECTUTE

to be done with it the poetic scam

of youth and trifling with sounds

anointments of illicit deities whose

wary whereabouts cannot be certain

longing for that season of ignorance

when language itself was incomplete

a sequence of rules to be memorized

before setting forth on paper ships

across the famous wading pond between

Greece and Asia the polymorphous

waters both shedding and reflecting

the great imagery of the sky in flux

wounds brought about by noise and

inflection tools of thought half-formed

lapses of time and moments when

day's reversal was possible the stone

and buttress of the fading library

trees and grass and shadows mourning

silently the impending passage that

leads south to the wars between man

and man isolation divorce and grief

letters arriving from the front that

inform nothing void and abscess

of heavens pouring down their mud

headlines streaked with omissions

and doubt to be able to return to

school having learnt math lessons
or pitfalls of rhetoric and looking
askance at the girls in their uniforms
of piety and license *them* the subject
of all poetry ! to deny that and versify
about anything else is lies and madness
one never really gets home again by
nightfall and the stars sparkling green
in the insane moment of true-love
if one could hold everything in check
disregarding earth's motion and polarity
and remain eternally the first poet *ever*
running to the mill where planets are born
from chaff and denial and bruiting epic
in long fields of hazy summers gone
alas and woe constant sorrow meddling
with fate looking for the right phrase
metonymy and metaphor the ancients
with their illegible books of dream-lore
to sleep realizing only half will ever be
enough to know and to learn to die
discarding years of hand-script notes
burning texts and hills of dialect writ
and scrap abjuring adolescence its
fate of automobile and alcohol
speed and grace and death

04-12-22

ODE TO CLAIRE BIRNBAUM

in the heart of the Vedas *my handsome*
winsome Johnny a voice a wan face
emerging from the window of obscurity
and how many years of forgotten legend ?
the burden of memory piled up by decades
there is no present tense worth fading
no almagest nor grimoire to consult
no stars to count steering by the astrolabe
just the penance of love's open wound
always and forever in the song of cycles
drop by drop the asphodel and paths
so dark there is no way but night's fork
that parts no sooner does the torchlight
shed its beam and fore and aft the hills
close their shuttered dialects and apse
ear struggles to recall the rules of meter
the gradation of sounds from zoom to
utter silence the heat of swarming bees
shaping asterisks of dusky air and high
before the first reckoning of noise in
swirling ferment of galaxies long dead
a roar of mental lunations a word
perhaps taking shape in the mind's lair
signs and portents of the light to come

breathing syllables the tryst of tongues
then boy meets girl and music brightens
the atmospheres and learning is to twine
the rope ascending to celestial spheres
springtime comes but once ! plum and
cherry perfume the winds that blow
from directions no number can explain
maps of sky clouds forlorn antiquities
of a single sonant buzzing in the blossom
to feel this moment has come and gone
before it can be perceived sorrows alone
account for passing lives and obscurities
not knowing today where they all are
shadowy brides and fellows at the bar
a round of drinks physics and cups
the rote of verse that extends for miles
vedic mantras eyes wide open to death
oncoming vehicles of ether and fog
sounding horses and spinning flames
the king of chariots ! fainted in the entry
head turned to stone still speaking
oracular stuff about the milky way and
uncountable souls that have vanished
in the small hour between yesterday and
now *my handsome winsome Johnny*
04-13-22

THE SECRET OF LIFE

it never happened the brokerage between
him and her blustery episodes traversing
snowfall and sunflower the lambent sun
in its Greek alphabet reclining over a music
of depths and seasonal disappearances
the halls darkened the folios mislaid
not words but muffled sounds footsteps
going downstairs to the Talmud and other
grammatical paraphernalia the stars and their
zodiacal houses signs and syllables in Old middle
Egypto-Chaldean text and madness forefront
the flood ! sand and more sand drowning
the universe for one night only introduced
to sex and the astrolabe at the same time
and poetry a great misadventure to describe
noise and particles falling at the speed of light
from a preterit heaven molded and seized
by the rapid hands of a demon wearing the mask
of a tender pronoun a skirt and blouse and
hair-pins in the mirror and the sleep of bees
in their mausoleum of gravel and mutiny
how loud the vacuum ! I am gone to love !
a campus with its ruins of brick and Platonism
twin factors of the cocktail hour when memory
is just a footnote to a labyrinthine conversation
notes struck high ! five o'clock death of the matador

sleaze of professors at the Banquet and sophists
and misanthropes declaring an end to Learning
the movie theater owes everything to Vivaldi
on a date the mismatched pair moon over the décor
lapsed from the painted ceiling where the mother
of Apollo and Artemis slowly vanishes in ether
don't touch ! don't remember ! drink ! drink !
soon everything collapses from mind and
hospitals open their derricks to fossil entrants
schoolboys with isosceles triangles and x-rays
prattling in an unknown dream-tongue
fix in the arm ! sheets and broken parallels
the twins on their witless wheel of paradise
and who will rescue the damsel ? Socrates ?
the book is over the reunion a farce the divorce
and the friends who flew in from the Lake
how small everything seems with its myrmidons
and radio-contestants with faulty knowledge
of the cosmos in its Italian dialect
the sun and its terrifying black homophone !
I recall clearly the entry in the catalog
where birth and death dates are in *italics*
the renown and lessening shadow of her body
under a bridge of unpunctuated hexameters
it all seems to have never really happened
the kiss the song the swoon the faint

04-13-22

AN AUTOBIOGRAPHICAL FOOTNOTE

as recorded never did most anything of own volition

spontaneity of the gods truculent and absent of mind

opinions about the theogony of Hesiod abjured

in column B only the left-wing supports holding

a fabulous day just once occurred all blossoms

and Appalachian spring driving by remote through

the fragrant dark to an episode of bankrupt religion

the controversy wasn't as much over age as love

at a premature stage and the riot of unnamed stars

crashing through the noosphere and avenues running

out of control past midnight and jazz and polyphonic

techniques applied to painting the short stay in a psych ward

and the doctors unimpressed no talent but for what

the right ear hears and declaiming Latin hexameters

to a brick column still smoking after the siege of Troy

more than ten cities one laid upon the other wafer thin

and compositions in stage fright and alcohol hitch-hiking

to the old south where the dead still hold trysts in

a shower of magnolia blossoms the song the rant the talk

machine-gun fast as the statues bolt out of their space

learning to use the right Platonic dialect and after

what seems like a few decades settled into a routine

and married with kids and a job and pasted to the ceiling

a map of the cosmos before the Big Bang and nature's

appropriate phonetic decay the holiday suit and reaction

to the totemic version a poem a day lunch with the angels

noontime like a bomb of light and louder than raffia

falling from the top of the Empire State and books and

titles of books without pagination and paragraphs

all in blank and the spirit that moves us and foremost

the unfinished epic called Pantograph after the discovery

of Spain and other islands of the East Indies the use

of Hindi to burrow beneath the outer layer of thought

millions of messages undecoded from the Rig Veda

becoming archaic and tender with grief the sorrowing

between hospitals and prescriptions for Nirvana

a hollow sense that nothing has really been achieved

and the morphology of memory a skeletal beauty

gauze and ether and the issue of gravity in its purity

descending the seas and shoals and cataracts Oh why !

deaths in mimeograph and *italics* and finality of knees

working shoes belittled hands iota and subscript

explain nothing utter futility of the Library and night

with its various illegible constellations of scripts

and emphasis on the penultimate hieroglyph and

Isis yes towering enormous shadowy mysterious as ink

distilled in the unlabeled laboratory where dreams are

performed and the high-school yearbook resuscitated

and the burials unfathomable as the orthography of sand

and I am here still wishing someone a successful life

bountiful with arms full of bouquets and budding

all hues and the dark taking me by the ankles and

reclining sleep in grass the inexplicable distance

04-14-22

KALENDA MAIA !

Kalenda maia
Ni fueills de faia
Ni chans d'auzell ni flors de glaia
Non es qe.m plaia ...

     Raimbaut de Vaqueiras

as I lay there sick and in a swoon a fate came to me
dressed as angel after the fall and deeper the voice I heard
darker my brain from light was cast aside until delved
into the bottoms my conscience became as starless night
no moon to dispel what I could no longer read and sorrow
and grief as gifts were at my reach hands and shapes
borrowed from a previous life a noise of echoes in tongues
long since abandoned sounds I perceived and syllables
a rant of prayers without sense a meaningless litany
what could I know of the waking and the morrow ?
yet shrouded in cloths of gloom and attitude an advance
of feet a hierarchy of bulletins from a lexicon of signs
archaic tabulations stone initials or steles set up to mark
a road inward to a place where silence and its double
inert matter struggle to feign life in subsets of grammar
and diagram the relentless authority to weigh and die
how much memory was left how little oblivion remained
as cities appeared great and fragile dust and smoke
and palaces half erected and gardens overrun by insects
whose enormous nocturnal orchestra stretched the ear
beyond comprehension into smatterings of dialects

of phantoms and effigies of reason and history books
ink and its immense subsidiaries of sky and atmosphere
clouds came to the glass and pleaded for entry and gods
who had never been born loomed hovering above the water
about to release auguries and ovations small-print details
about salvation and judgments and instructions as to what
to do should I wake again to another existence a being
of lesser concord and spell a semi-automatic weapon
of thought coruscating in a renewed cosmos of feelings
the thing dwelling within mind the shapeless yawning
extent of space outside of space youth eternal grass and
rotations of alphanumeric symbols and no place to lay
the stone and rest watching collision of particles and size
height and illusion the disremembered moments on a lawn
pairing shadow to body and reciting lessons of chemistry
and rhetoric music ! then from the long coma in which I lay
a satellite of delusion and distortion I slowly came to
in a bed of reeds by a rushing water near a shade of trees
a spirit wrestling with substance to become free of language
pronoun and mask disunities of motion and yearning
the path ! it lay before me if only I had the steps to take
to resume this dream of existence and imperfection
I have gone through all the phases head heavy as a rock
and bow bidding farewell to these verses of melancholy
a suite of glossolalia aphasia and love's old refrain yet
it all comes together Dante the Wake and *Kalenda Maia* !

04-15-22

DEEPER THE DIALECT DARKER THE SOUL

the rotting underwood of consternation

a street that only goes half way there

married to a sepulcher ! the *already* of premonition

how many hoods to cover the diphthong of absence

to her whom I never see the darkling one

over the seas of memory in a chasuble of ink and sorrow

from such spring the roots of poetry the blaspheme

and the startled bird-song of oblivion

high on its wing of tribulation and strife

I note and strike writing the furious sounds

sent to me in sleep the lavender chorale of *primavera*

was I ever more than a wayward pronoun

a pronunciation of something buried deep

in a text of redundancies of ear and fable

ants ! labyrinthine yards of unseen empire

and suns that circle blotting the skies of reverie

a child a swarm of bees a hunting horn in the hills

this and more foretell the ancient spell of doom

how is today no more lamp than the acrostic of *death*

a sample of noises baroque and elaborate in the nave

where I tarry the *other* self of myself

a digit and warning that the future has been erased

envelopes arrive full of hair such a plangent device

to make melancholy the druid emotions dawn brings

to bear and to drive ! satellite motions to curtail

breath and semblance of language and memory

details bit by bit of heat and the exchanged rings

being pronounced man and wife to no one

a tombstone a flag marking the start of grass

the leaves in the back begin again their lament

Beatrice ! secret idyll of woman repetition

of shadow and form marble effulgence

let me say it another way : O !

04-15-22

AN EPISTLE FROM THE LETHE

I speak to my friends new and old

dead or alive visible or invisible thus

I open discourse to those who cannot hear

whose lives are past dissent whose breath

and light whose very limbs heart and soul

are the stuff of fiction or memory which is

the greater fiction the illusory existentialism

of borderline cities of Mexicos without a past

of whiff and whim the total infancy of words

to all whom I never met this is for you

to puzzle over to question why to disturb

stone and rock to dispose of gravel and pools

midnights in search of identities of repetition
and rotation to cause music to be sounded on
its irreversible gong and chime and sweeten
the only plausible hour there is somewhere
between the Mayo Clinic and the bus-stop
with its suspended clock for whom time and space
are simply notches on a wooden stick tossed
high into the air for a dog to retrieve if that
dog with its multiple personalities will ever
come back to life and I am especially calling
out to the eight thousand girls who were
born on the Buddha's birthday or so the Pali
Canon seems to claim a matter for auditors
to explore or implore the deities as well who
sought safe conduct after death and willing
to reply though no address in the cosmos
exists under that name and date the parallel
streets about to finally meet in this fundamental
epistle to whom I am appealing rhetoricians
and orators alike effigies and phantoms and
whoever else I can summon to mind before my own
flame goes out come rain or shine and songs that
have their effect on the brain like alcohol
or speed and denizens of the underworld souls
comets meteors nameless planets plunging
through the soil of the atmospheres into Pluto's

sparkling dungeon and by the banks of the Lethe

where blues master Little Walter blows his brains

out with a feeling that is difficult to replicate and

so dear reader in absentia I am willing to dispose

of this pronoun tear off my mask become really

nobody at all whom you will not recall as

an encounter in your lives a linguistic attitude

a charade in *italics* reserved for Saturday

night dates at the movies or at a dance-hall

jitterbug boogie-woogie lindy hop fox-trot

two step and finally yes and the enigmatically

so-called end of this application for anonymity

thank you in advance for not replying

and a fine morning it is with rain and all

that we remain *unknown* is the best

and comes Mary Lou fresh from the grave

as young as when we first met and wasn't that

a time a dance and a ringing in the air not

knowing where the sound goes after it dies

04-16-22

THE STORY OF LIFE

divine child you turned your back

and everything fell apart the light

in the attic with its model airplanes

the stuff that surrounds the universe

the small sequence of rooms leading

from the beginning of grass to the oval

where the sun forms its black homophone

all the cherished digits of memory

the songs and wordless humming of

the mothers in their tender blindness

always ignorant and the fossil beings

stirring in the dark to wake if possible

blade held to lamp shoes scattered across

the western half of the empyrean the loud

and impossible vowel of being coming forth

and time to lace up straighten out assume

some sort of pose eke out a living bear

the freight on the hope that memory

will somehow withstand the cathedrals

of noise and pounding up and down

excess of motion and gravity pronouns

to be worn and suits buttoned up and

masks dusted off the stage a ploy mere

baggage of nonsense to pretend this is

how it's done and exchange vows glove

and ring the smaller hills charged with
dialect and distance and whom will you
greet at the new doorway and what city
is that you are drawing so illusory pure
hallucination of avenues and roadways
planned and perfected only to be erased
come tomorrow when leaving all that
behind a promise of drugs and warfare
and hell itself next to the gasoline pump
you will deny and excoriate and aggrandize
fueled by the desire to be a perfect entity
it's all myth and make-up playing the droll
partner of a shadow knowing it's only
death on the ox-cart burdened with
leather and fancy cloths bound for the
bottom-lands where they mete out
punishments and derricks and horses
that operate by levers the mechanics
of failure over and over will do nothing
to resolve fate and the empty shells
hand-to-hand combat with the self
having tried the alternate compounds
the assertions that another life persists
somewhere on the moon or in its razed
suburbs you will defend skin and verb
and antimony the dark matter you are
language and enigma stuttering sleeper

took the wrong turn on the pike thumb

and wrist deft application and air darker

as night descends swiftly to take you

this moment was always there from

the start even when you were playing

just a kid in the schoolyard looking

scared of something terrible refulgent

half hidden in the bushes and scraping and

yelling the others too already dead with

you in that swift indefinable obscurity

that takes everyone unawares

"a dark brick building that is no more"

04-17-22

THE HELL-BOOK

cannot go on just being ourselves

there must be more to the illusion than this

a brocaded finery tassels crimson hanging

as if from a cloud and the mud below acres and miles

of it their reflections hard to discern in the density

cannot keep assuming there is another chapter

of light or that breath will go on and on

a page at a time decipherments of language

the detective at the door face hidden

asking more questions than we had answers

a bell-ringing announced distance at five PM

drugs and retribution the kids ganging the windows

where death displays its haunting trinkets

stuff to wear and go crazy over the drinks too

the streaming live version of existence

two fingers from the platinum leaf

and the poets who cannot get published

and looking askance at a sky diminished

by a hundred fold since yesterday the astrologer

gauging fate by the number of vowels in the lesson

how many have disappeared since last we counted

the soldier-boys just went daft from memory

shells and good riddance to the enemy in his ditch

we have totally botched history and its ancillary lies

the exams failed the traffic lights went bonkers

horns sounding intermittently louder each time

hail-stones of coagulated blood and thunder

green implosions stone-ears a manufactured pronoun

parading between asterisks and the gored matador

poetry ! fixation of meter and death's similitude

rigidity of clauses and determination of grades

metaphor and Etruscan graveyard etiquette

painted the air with sublime representations of wingéd

creatures an assault on reason the beds lined up

against the wall and sobbing and children dying

machinery of impulse and resonance

everything must have happened simultaneously
the ruined harvest the drought followed by floods
and more floods casting gravel by the fist-full
at the passing windows and haunted as ever
by the stage-play showing Zeus bawling like a baby among
the birds of prey with faces of movie actresses
cosmetics and asbestos delineations of beauty
Fra Angelico on a stool contemplating suicide
virtually every sin in the book exposed to the kids
taking what they can and driving their cars
off the cliff with glee and the waters below
six hundred waters deeper and darker the drowning
devastations and pulse still faintly beating
can I get a witness ? a hand emerging clasping
the metal unit of identity and tides going out
so small the evocations of ivy and myth
here was stranded the Bull and here inside the pool
did ink increase its matter becoming great
as a book that can never be read and the heavens
imploring and walking on their knees and suffixes
appended to their navels to remind them of birth
and so on and so on the immensities of oblivion
here was mortality and its fane of ruin and wrack
must be a difference that sets immortality off
from the tempest of human emotions
more than being ourselves what else is there ?

04-18-22

THE ORIGINS OF DEATH

and finished baiting the gods with illusions of circularity
those of us wood-dwellers who are not used to chariots
nor to the dust and gore of battle with foot-men
proceeding beneath the great yawning skies half-conscious
but it is the habit of language that is most disconcerting
the elements and invisible properties of sound to the ear
nuances of darkness the ancient recollections of rock
and aloft petrified birds and the signs of warning and
despair beneath each cloud the solitary roaming of
breath and plaint the disguised augury of nothing to come
tracing with wet fingertip the wind's course southward
errant and wild and listening for the rattle of wheels
for the cry of osprey or kestrel for waves emerging
somber and threatening from the depths outside the realms
of light and to sleep midst blackened trunks and the shouts
of ancestral deities a looming mass of air gathering
as if to smother the descent of each man of us confused
the discordant noise of unseen beings in the undergrowth
a fear to never wake again should sleep overcome by noon
and horses untethered waiting in the glade the promise
of sunrise of altars of distance and smoking rituals
memorizing unintelligible syllables meant to invoke and
appease some greater entity with lessons of proximity
the very enigma of glances between persons unmasked

the raw and yet sweet graze of palm on cheek the fire

within enveloping the heart and leaping with amaze

into the hour of spray and verdure the silent step of

the goddess somewhere behind us a prompting of tongues

and moving moving into the marble glare of day-break

whenever discourse begins a doubt that anything

will ever come to completion the mysteries of the eye

the freight and gravity of the sun shifting its gold assonance

toward the western hills where undiscovered cities lurk

paths and interferences medley hum and buzz of thought

to harness energy and whispering between the leaves

an emotion to be great to charge through the density

with verses of unexplored weight and the breadth of time

a limitless moment like the edge of sex and the spark

of union between bodies and the seraphic emblem

that ignites the agreement of pronouns diaphanous as

the mouth of the world and it is for the others hearing

the maze of insect empires or the swiftness of wings

to comprehend if possible the secret meaning of things

incandescence and stillness the head turns to stone

and eternity takes flight in the discharge of death

04-19-22

VARIATIONS ON A LINE BY BHAVABHUTI

"has the third eye of the black-red god opened wide ?"

when flowers become crepuscular and dust motivates

a resurgence in gravity and time manifests

weapons of never-before destruction shining

like rain-wet lotus petals in the urgency of the hour

it is everywhere and nowhere at once the irreversible instant

the topical cream the comb the lipstick the mascara

the mirror that reveals a soul separate from itself

noises greater than the birth of stone and winds

rushing through the ear-hole of fate the smaller

inches dividing the sections of a single moment

sandstorms and ant-hills grapevines clamoring

to break the window-pane and enter a salon

the color of musk and death and clouds mushrooming

on all eighteen horizons how different language is !

if only the world could be reduced to a simple dimension

to one glyph alone representing a forest deer

about to swallow a pool of immaculate water

and yet we wander in our pivotal circle kids

snared by the illusion of memory going backwards

through centuries of swart and brilliant thoughts

I was here first ! rumors and errors of grammar and

method diagrams of cities that never existed shimmering

with a traffic of weevil and midge bearing faces

of adolescents bound to die before mid-term

and what of the deity who wears duplicate even triplicate

identities like sleeves of light or airborne seeds

it is poetry ! first and foremost long page-size

word-compounds describing acts of intimacy and

terror and echoes of zing and boom and shrill weapons

the world devastated repeatedly by wars against itself

dance of destruction the multiple feet of the three-eyed god

swarming with phases of womanhood and lunacy

how can there ever be understanding of the sacred ?

we mount ideograms and ride phantom steeds into hills

where enigma and oracle involve other universes

sound outside of sound ! silence limited by whiteness !

every time we dial a number a voice recurs

resonance and sleep occupying the same vowel

we can never graduate from high-school !

ampersands and diacritical antiquities the unfathomable

in skies painted yesterday by Michelangelo

it is all zoom and text and threadbare realities

of the microchip and cathode ray

we have never been here ! we exist over *there* !

04-20-22

ME LLAMO JUANITO

> *"Hail Pepi this, pure art thou,*
> *pure is thy double, pure is thy power*
> *among the spirits, pure is thy soul*
> *among the gods"—Text of Pepi I*

a long time ago there was a man in Mexicali
who taught me how to shout my name as loud as possible
I shouted *Me llamo Juanitooooooooooooooooooooooo!!!!!!!!*
I am told you could hear this as far away as the Mayo Clinic
since then I have inhabited this echo like a mirror
the other side shouted *Me llamo*
Pepitoooooooooooooooooooooooo!!!!!!!
that was Joe in his early Toltec phase shy diffident
in a ragged striped t-shirt worn on days of Reformation
either one of us equally disposed to unbearable silences
the semblance of death in an underlined word or
the *italics* and representation of memory in a pool
the size and color of the sky when it isn't there
autumns came and went and the exclamation marks
of our singular shouts persisted like small lunations
clouds or remote bee-swarms imitating flamenco guitars
how could we have grown up so swiftly?
the maps we designed still float somewhere in the noosphere
tattered and worn with the fading names of wives
girlfriends or goddesses who dwell hidden in motels
just off South Broadway and cornfields too and

the matter of the universe and its reversal of fortune

the pyramids of *Sol y Luna* exaggerated by consonant clusters

easing the restrictions of thought and lunacy

Joe ! that song *You belong to me* goes on and on

in and out of light spectra and thousands of plunging

undiscovered galaxies refugees of a summer night where

in a fluorescence high in the northern sky our shouted names

coruscate nostalgic flickering Mexican phonemes

since then a havoc and tantrum of distances has upended

all that ever was -- waves and overturned boats and hands

from nowhere bearing signet rings of hieroglyphic noise

we too will escape the parameters of sound

divorced from pronoun and envy to enter the underworld

where Osiris and his double wading in a phantom water

wait for us wait for each of us either one

the half of the other in weight and destiny and nearby

among the reeds a makeshift coffin-bark lists tilting

south toward lands of shadow and echo

you and me, Bro' shouting

!!!!!!

Me llamo Juanito
Me llamo Pepito

04-20-22

DEATH IS THE SOUND WE HEAR
WHEN WE'RE NOT LISTENING

why does no one read these poets anymore ?
are their voices too loud too shrill too hush too brogue ?
a word is a tangle of noise the thought of echo
aphasia is clearly in the ascendant reaching sky
cosmic quarters the parts of the body enunciated
threads woven through eye and ear turned to stone
blanks between the lines and voids replace meaning
salvation is in the turn-style ! hearing substitutes value
they are on the corner being rowdy and anxious
those adolescents of music and meter the very rain
of their patter the tinny fusion of antiquities with
post-modern mumbo jumbo syllabic claptrap
fission and heat of dementia the very fruit of idealism
they are rhyming and jamming and hip-hop
radios of jargon and metaphor but where is the song ?
put in parenthesis mind alters its stutter perilous
dreams of antithesis and black matter
the universe of parallels before the Big Bang
so much and little else to consider on this May day
in the fright-dwelling of time and all of mankind
on the edge of the abyss pest and warfare reigning
allusions to the metronome and understanding
erased with a dose of amnesia and imperfect statuary

no one reads these poets anymore mostly just because

and they are insouciant brash verbatim helter skelter

their circularity goes back to the Upanishads !

here sit the demons who existed before the gods

they are evil and denounce correct speech

they lack method and spread discord through the body

with assemblage of grammar and misreading

they swell death with hunger and simply wait

they cannot leave high school they are in suspension

required to memorize verses no one has ever written

hyaline solutions retribution numbness in the brow

soon dialectic and hills of longing will occur

afterthoughts to memory and its divisive skies

long afternoons in the library reading Book of the Dead

will there ever be any other way out ?

words words words the humiliation of lexicons

we cannot last we were meant to expire

silence

04-22-22

PHOTO OF MAX ON HORSEBACK

for Marilla

how melodramatic now there is nothing

snippets of a biography riding horseback

until summer loses its hills of heat and longing

and we are at the Grand Canyon tossing

the beloved one in the form of ashes into

Nature's rugged beauties chasms and voids

a universe parallel to this one where he

rides the horse back into an unsuspecting

childhood a maze of inferno and schooldays

in a city built on a bridge of water and under

the rushing conduits trains of noise rush

bearing corpses and more corpses to Chinatown

how does the amalgam of sweetness and light

so suddenly turn into an ambulance ?

renaming the streets or pretending the curve

doesn't exist where space and time intersect

and volumes of Sanskrit and petty forwards

to books of poetry what a riot of illusion !

we were not made to endure only to experience

drums and flutes and insects that zing happy

that air exists and clouds swarming above

skipping and hopping on sidewalks and

going crazy with a perpetual melody what !

life with its strings of ABC and boomerangs

the very notion of breathing forever ?

tall in the saddle defiant despite massive

efforts of mystery to erase the present

captured forever in Technicolor radiance

Max holding the reins imperturbable

in the face of eternity's awesome labyrinth

04-22-22

FOOTNOTE TO BRHDARANYAKA UPANISAD

for Bob Ness

"From the unreal / lead me to the real!"
and it is precisely from darkness we emerge
perilous passage confusion of noise and letters
someone whose distance is incalculable shouting
in vowels borrowed from infinity what little
difference between the coming and the going
in between there is no shelter from the unreal
and knocking on numerous doors and looking
askance for your own voice and thunder and
trembling of the airwaves and shooting fires
on high and scrapping illusions for deaths
multiple as the sleep of stone or ice and what
is remembered just as soon forgotten at the

first traffic light and you wait in rooms darker
than pre-dawn for a prescription or a label
to place on a bottle wandering from chair to
chair not recalling the name assigned to the
pronoun you are wearing isn't it strange how
one door is opened only to be locked again
from the inside where plural forms of water
and gravel involve centuries of grass growing
downwards to the south where dense whir
of machinery gags the muffled echo of statues
being taken from one life to the next a round of
breath and anticipation enigmatic moment
when everything is revealed instantaneously only
to be obscured in dumbstruck awe the unknown
a flower in the midst of chaos and rumination
of the stars whose wreckage comes to us as
a baleful light one fervent august night
when archaic children in our bodies scour
the shifting careless map of the galaxies looking
for just one single spot a dot or asterisk
on which the universe depends for meaning
then do we plunge from ecstasies into pools
of eternal night lost to one another hand and
mind all patterns dissolved of intent and style
no cry no leaf no energies of fading time
only the remote puzzling oracle of sound

04-23-22

INSPIRED BY VERLAINE

bird in flight my little book of memories

lost and lorn the seas below and vast the blanks

between unwritten words a melancholy that

does not abate a summer session in fields

long cemented over a thrill when rhapsody

of bees in literary swarm comes into sight

longing that lasts forever for the unknown

hospice for the broken-hearted who cannot

read the invisible verses of my little book

cupola of clouds and shelter from the rains

paragraphs of little use and fragments like

rocks jutting from the shore and waters as

violent as passions can endure the sequences

of life the ways littered with loss and yearning

come what may the end is sure no nestled

comfort only grief the unstitched syllables

that punctuate the untitled poems of this

small book of verse this unpublished tome

that wings its way unconscious soaring

blindly into the sun's blazing homophone as

if to acquire some taste of fame and oblivion

in the endless burning of its memories

04-24-22

X MARKS THE SPOT

"War, one war after another ..."
        E. Pound

the finality of language on the court-house lawn
shadows of future skyscrapers and abandoned libraries
the French medieval epic the Dolce stil novo missing
parts paginations gone astray tables reversed indexes
and thumb-prints gangster editions of the Comedy
read aloud in the basement with microfilm copies
a life alphabetizing wrong-way streets and obituaries
where is Fifth Avenue today now that Lennon is dead ?
remember to forget the morning it all capsized
Latin epigraphs unfinished and *a capella* on the stoop
hot wringing summer sheets in the yellowish air
the eventuality of the least likelihood suddenly Bang !
rushing down brownstone streets to an emergency room
elevators don't work windows clamped shut can't breath
without a machine and the medical personnel like zombies
looking for the switch that turns the blood flow off
chamber music ! the viola player has been dead for years
yet his Mozart is the Bible itself a mooring to waters
parted by the stroke of a high-C note the distance between
mellifluous and mephitic as for the others with tremolo
and vibrato in suspense while the mid-morning havoc
stretches out into years and years into decades wretched
calendar dates regrettable folio manuscripts with

blurred water-marks spots and echoes of lost words

music is the faded reference to infinity falling asleep

and the dense woods the irretrievable byways paths

disguised by nettles thorns thick underbrush nearby

the grotto which is the entrance to Pluto's finite realm

the chasm that resonates with cries of treason and broken

promises the chalks and whittled twigs and stitches

the cicatrix of mind ! I remember going up and down

the shady avenue with a friend and then the wars began

religion against religion unidentified gods the plumbers

and electricians who can fix nothing and the house itself

mystery and fane of the Enigma sphinx and puzzled

phantom quizzing each other about the Origins and

nothing comes of it only the commas and asterisks

that punctuate the ear listening for that last vowel

eerily floating through the gas and ether of eternity

04-25-22

VOICE MIND BREATH

the pin-up on the fading gasoline wall

hearkens back to a time when the universe

was just a thought before growing up

decisions and reluctance the void is all around

its shape and content fill the world with light
streaked and abjured by darkness the remainder
of time measured by a thumbnail and the cries
of living and dead alike morph into absence
and delusion of speech all around a statue
of noon heat and effervescence a rumor
of nightfall of things that cannot ever occur
memory of a cave of motion and gravity
what is the cause for despair ? error of being
chain-cycle of distances perceived only in sleep
the looming axis of space slowly spinning
in the antechamber of mind and loud
and irrevocable the sounds that litter the ceremony
fires offered to deities who have no presence
guardians of the eighteen quarters and
cities of unimaginable splendor buried
in the mountain where thought becomes a dialect
centuries on the wane summers deposited
like stolen gold in lawns of evening and
childhoods swift and immeasurable as grass
who determines term limits ?
waters that run through nocturnal air
moons in roundelay and leaf and breath alike
the shining in midst of chaos ! millennia longing
to return but to where ?
04-26-22

"NOTHING'S GONNA CHANGE MY WORLD"
(Lennon/McCartney)

then does a man wither away and die
not remembering sky is body of the mind
and waters and fires and all his deeds are naught
a fixed sphere cannot exist ! he takes to the field
of youth and counts the grasses as if they were
pages of his unwritten book and is proud
though he has accomplished nothing and the stars
that prowl around the fatal nocturnal realms
speak to him loud and tell him to desist !
a bird in flight is the reckoning of his thought
unable to stay in place restless among rock fragments
a poet a dreamer an idler in the midst of noise
he brings home some money and builds a roof
and marries and cannot stay put and learns
a little about the gamble of the gods and their
size and attributes but cannot put in place
the letters of their names and is futile in regard
to the knowledge required to understand
the limits of the sea the borders of land the heights
of mountain and speech and is corrupt in
his phonology and stammers and utters nonsense
like a statue cursed with identity and pronoun
nowhere to turn in the shortening days

his breath will soon become inanimate and
brief until like a candle in the wind he goes out --
there were those days of flickering and small
joys which he accounted as immortal moments
eternity ! a dip in the black pool of sagacity
and coming up for air all was a dazzle a Spanish
idiom a fluttering of colored skirts in a courtyard
far from the moment of birth and then Bang !
like a hammer fallen from the clouds he stumbled
something like a spear-tip penetrated him
from temple to temple and hearing someone
call his name *Achillles !* he tasted dust and
left the world of breathless sunsets

04-27-22

THOU ART THAT

the sound that follows man is an echo of reality
up in the sun or gazing from the moon or hidden
in the violent topographies of wind or rain the maze
of realities no one fully comprehends and the sand
and gravel the multiple grasses of the hill the water
of reflection which is the unknown sky's shadow
pool of the glade where spotted deer gather
to drink and in seeing their resemblances ripple

become *other* in a reality that has nothing to do

with the immense invisibility where we subsist

in overwhelming details of mirage and recall --

do other voices beckon do clouds work a sort of triumph

does the lightning bolt conceal a mortal destiny unwritten

and sealed before its time do hours shed their clocks

and walls of sleep merge with endless dialects of distance ?

youth alone is the true realm of noise and fleeting chaos

rumors of life unending and love supreme the sublime

and nonsensical moment of irretrievable poetry

mountebank and troubadour seer and charlatan pose

in a three-piece suit that adorns the graduation photo

the rest is dross of responsibility and make-believe

drudgery of mendacity and promotion the job

of enduring day after day until the prize of death

is the reunion of all realities the *Brahma* and mask

that define the *soul* unpunctuated breath that eludes

how is it we can never quite grasp the *whole* yet

go on seeking in grammar and text of spatial voids

trying to read scripts of stellar disinformation

denying and affirming that *this* is *that* ?

furious pronouns of the *id* ! loss is unendurable

the day sets with its pallid final sun a homophone

blackened by constant grief the puzzles of memory

skeletal remoteness of a mountain perceived just once

on the margins of birth and knowledge

tat tvam asi

04-28-22

THE RUMOR OF LANGUAGE

lizard of the strengths of sleep !

rope of sand that ties the world to insomnia

imitations of air and emphasis of wind in *italics*

luxuries of the absent clouds of memory

how can it be the eye is the clue to being ?

to sing in the key of delta the pharaonic mysteries

somewhere between the archaic lyric crevice

and the renewed thought of osmosis and perishing

whenever the channel runs its course among the sheets

the pliant discords of the feminine plural of water

the vastly finite mind in its imperfect design

that wakes while still asleep for months on end

the moons that circle insanely the day's earliest child

who goes roaming among dark grasses looking

for the glass hand that holds his shadow captive

how many times have we lost ? salvation is nowhere near

the ancient seers the devils and the placid ruminants

who devour the flaming ramparts of the universe

offer nothing can no longer speak and share

but one eye but one ear and a single mouth to silence

it is error that governs the cosmos and chaos

is at the heart of order & we struggle to understand

what tiny virtue what speck of dust what consonant

sustains the part of outer space that belongs to the sun

the rest is veering out of line toward horizons of dialect

as time runs out the weary wheel wobbles to the left

the spear-tip and the greaves that designate heroic acts

are phantom realities in the long hour of make-believe

literature is nothing more than linguistic specimens

words and their fancy acts of retaliation !

poetry remains an enigmatic rune hidden in an apiary

hemispheres of pyramids ! the brother whose death

has come to mean that language has lost all sense

04-29-22

IMAGINATION : AN ACCOUNT

... come to naught there by the eddying

rills of the gentle stream by midday when

the sun's rays are hottest and from on high

not even the lauded immortals are of any use

face down in the muddy turf expired the unnamed

hero of written word juvenile and anxious

ere night clasp him by the knees hurtling him

downward into the sumptuous but dark palace

of Hades in a confusion the day's breaking news

and from the library spread the heralded glory

of the contest between imaginary heroes the full

pedigree of either warrior filled with literary

promise did I then turn the page scribbled

with hallowed syllables stolen from the Sibyl's

archaic rant day-dream of eternal adolescence

in my chariot of metaphysical flame the clouds

and thunder of prophesy threatening the yearbook

and skies magnificent with distance and hue

how I yearned to be *other* the acoustic variant

of some half-conscious bard torn from the routines

of his daily hexameters inscribing in the ether

the tendentious nonsense of the world's last

great epic or at least a prolegomena to

the thought-bank of a novel poetic experiment

involving the loves and attributes the consonants

and shared vowels the accent and tonic heights

of a language barely past its seventeenth year

hunh ? me the exaggerated twin of luminescence

and alcohol stuttering aimlessly with accolades

shod with meter and hoof of Olympus the one

and if not the other *the* only author of invisible texts

the writ and chasm of invaded ballrooms whose

existence justified every Saturday night and alloyed

and smitten with song the effort to dance and praise

as never before the Muse ! cosmetics and cherry coke

the fabled drug-store the lapse in time and memory

the ingredients for everlasting fame wasted

in long dalliance with nymphs whose mere presence

is death and death alone the rites and strophes

of the endless and barely commenced poem

imagination

04-30-22

MAKE YE PRAYER TO KING ZEUS SON OF CRONOS

who have reached far into the depths of Tartarus

sulfurous miasma in search of their abandoned husks

wavering intellect and memory slowly devolving mists

who bereft of name and pronoun and sleeping in the skin

of oblivion thousand-armed dreams phantoms and echoes

assail the drifting mind and what of language and its

corrupt phonologies and the efforts of sound to *mean*

something despite the circularity of unwritten texts

and of kings and battles and the polyphasic poetry

of runes and hieroglyphs the sunrise of consonants

disturbed seas of the unconscious the swelling tides

lunations and idiolects if the soul could only swim !

to employ right sense to strings of vowels and mantras

in the dawn of breath and trees surging animate

holy in the springtime of cosmic disorder and gods

to appeal and pray and set up altars of denial and
uproot the gardens of paradise ruminating on chaos
and its aesthetics of dynamite and light fossil planets
orientations of hills and dialects and sunsets without
direction when only south matters and the divinities
of the dead surrounded by organisms of history and
myth the junction of hand and noise and all error
which accrues from the rumor of life in ascension
do we but stop to surmise on extinction and parallels
of matter the great and yawning abyss of space in context
rushing futilities of flame and the stuttering utterances
of augurs and oracles situated on their islands of bitumen
and pitch the all-hell of existence within the plate-glass
window displays of mortal passage the bric-a-brac of
intent and love the fuming sleep between beings who
long to be perfect entities in the desperate round of rebirth
and dying each an alphabet of reunion only to be shattered
into songs and pyramids and treacherous Spanish sands
adrift alone amidst the shipwreck of untitled poems
man's small craft loosed into the maelstrom
swirl of nameless stars and endless waters
of infinite infinities

05-01-22

Poetry by Iván Argüelles

published by Luna Bisonte Prods:

THE UNFINISHED BREATH:
New Poems, Elegies, and Laments. V.1 [2023]

THE TRANSLATION TO HEAVEN
& Related Poems [2022]

IMMOBILITY - - Poetry [2022]

FIELD HOLLERS (with Solomon Rino) [2021]

TAMAZUNCHALE [2021]

THE SHAPE OF AIR FRAGMENTS [2021]

DIARIO DI UN OTTOGENARIO [2020]

TWILIGHT CANTOS [2019]

CIEN SONETOS [2018]

LAGARTO DE MI CORAZÓN [2018]

FRAGMENTS FROM A GONE WORLD [2017]

LA INTERRUPCIÓN CONVERSACIONAL [2016]

ORPHIC CANTOS [2015]

DUO POEMATA:
ILION—A TRANSCRIPTION
& ALTERTUMSWISSENSCHAFT [2015]

FIAT LUX [2014]

A DAY IN THE SUN [2012]

ULTERIOR VISIONS [2011]

Available at:

https://www.lulu.com/spotlight/lunabisonteprods